THE DAY OF
DELIVERANCE

THE DAY OF DELIVERANCE
BREAKING THROUGH BARRIERS TO A BETTER MARRIAGE

KELLY SIMMONS

THE DAY OF DELIVERANCE
Copyright © 2024 by Kelly Simmons

All rights reserved. Neither this publication nor any part of this publication may be reproduced or transmitted in any form or by any means, electronic or mechanical, including photocopying, recording or any information storage and retrieval system, without permission in writing from the author.

Unless otherwise indicated, scripture quotations are taken from the New King James Version®. Copyright © 1982 by Thomas Nelson, Inc. Used by permission. All rights reserved. • Scripture quotations marked (AMP) are taken from the Amplified® Bible, Copyright © 1954, 1958, 1962, 1964, 1965, 1987 by The Lockman Foundation. Used by permission. • Scripture quotations marked (NLT) are taken from the Holy Bible, New Living Translation, copyright © 1996, 2004, 2015 by Tyndale House Foundation. Used by permission of Tyndale House Publishers, Inc., Carol Stream, Illinois 60188. All rights reserved. • Scripture quotations marked (NASB) are taken from the New American Standard Bible®, Copyright © 1960, 1971, 1977, 1995, 2020 by The Lockman Foundation. All rights reserved. • Scripture quotations marked (RSV) are taken from the Revised Standard Version of the Bible, copyright © 1973 National Council of the Churches of Christ in the United States of America. Used by permission. All rights reserved worldwide. • Scripture quotations marked (BBE) are taken from the Bible in Basic English, which is in the public domain. • Scripture quotations marked (KJV) are taken from the Holy Bible, King James Version, which is in the public domain. • All Scripture marked with the designation "GW" is taken from GOD'S WORD®. © 1995, 2003, 2013, 2014, 2019, 2020 by God's Word to the Nations Mission Society. Used by permission.

ISBN: 978-1-4866-2468-3
eBook ISBN: 978-1-4866-2469-0

Word Alive Press
119 De Baets Street Winnipeg, MB R2J 3R9
www.wordalivepress.ca

Cataloguing in Publication information can be obtained from Library and Archives Canada.

CONTENTS

ACKNOWLEDGEMENTS — vii
FOREWORD — xiii
INTRODUCTION — xix

CHAPTER ONE
Restrained in Egypt — 1

CHAPTER TWO
I Have Seen Your Sorrow — 13

CHAPTER THREE
I Am Come to Deliver You — 23

CHAPTER FOUR
I Will Send You — 35

CHAPTER FIVE
Plagued with Opposition — 53

CHAPTER SIX
The Desert Season — 71

CHAPTER SEVEN
Believe the Good Report — 91

CHAPTER EIGHT
Taking Jericho — 105

CHAPTER NINE
Declaring the Victory — 123

ADDITIONAL SCRIPTURE CONFESSIONS — 137

ACKNOWLEDGEMENTS

I have many thanks to extend to those who have so graciously helped me throughout this book project. First and foremost, my Lord and Saviour, Jesus Christ. I was at the beginning, and continue to be, both amazed and exceedingly honoured at the great blessing and privilege to be given this work to write. Thank You, Lord, for Your grace and constant presence with me in writing this book. Truly it was You who brought it forth. Without You, it could not have been accomplished, for without You I am nothing. I love You. You are my everything. You are my all. Thank You for my marriage, my husband, and my family. Thank You for bringing us together, and thank You for *keeping* us together. Words are not enough to express my gratitude for Your unfailing love for me.

I would also like to thank my husband, Dale, who remained faithful in prayer for me as I sat at my computer day in and day out, read and reread the manuscript, and encouraged me all along the way. Thank you for allowing me to put our growth and struggles to paper without protest but with continuous support and encouragement. I love you so much—more than you know. You are my soulmate for life. I would choose no other man on earth to share my life with.

Next, I'd like to thank my mother, Sarah—or Momzie to me. Thank you for being such an outstanding example of what a wife should be. Although you didn't know it, I watched you through the years as you loved my daddy so sweetly and submissively. Truly you were a godly wife to him and a beautiful example to me, and you continue to be a mother to be proud of. Thank you also for coming when I called you to read the manuscript and make corrections for me. I wasn't sure who to call upon for that task. I'm so glad it was you. I love you.

To Pastor Cathy Ciaramitaro—author, mentor, friend. I've learned so very much from you. Thank you for giving me the opportunity to both step out and grow in the gifting of the Lord to teach. I remember sitting in your office when you gave me that very first opportunity. No pressure, lol! Thank you also for taking time out of your busy schedule to read this manuscript, for your mentorship and friendship over the years, and for your remarkable example of godly leadership. Your mentorship has been invaluable.

ACKNOWLEDGEMENTS

Last but certainly not least, Sis. Joyce Brown, Sis. Love. It was you that believed so strongly that God called me to preach that you told me to prepare a message and had me preach it to you over the phone to encourage me to step out for it in faith. It was you that God used to mentor me in my first steps of ministry, allowing me to teach the women's Bible study group. It was you that God used to tell me to write. Thank you for the years of pouring into my life. You are loved.

"Wisdom is the principal thing; therefore get wisdom. And in all your getting, get understanding." (Proverbs 4:7)

FOREWORD

"You will keep him in perfect peace, Whose mind is stayed on You, Because he trusts in You." (Isaiah 26:3)

When my husband and I first got married, we promised each other that, as we were to become one flesh (Genesis 2:24), we would give due diligence to becoming involved in each other's interests, particularly the ones we did not currently enjoy. For me, that meant watching and learning a game that I then despised—golf.

As a young girl, I became interested in a few sports because of my father's interests. He enjoyed most sports. Among his favourites were basketball, football, and, yes, golf, which I disliked the most. Why a person would want to walk around chasing a tiny white ball in the hot sun—and even, at times, the rain—was beyond me. But Daddy not only played the game—he also thoroughly enjoyed watching it on television as well.

Now basketball was a little different. We lived in East Lansing, Michigan when I was growing up, the home of the Spartans, which meant many days perched in the stands of Genesee Stadium, and that was all right by me. Those were the days of Magic Johnson. I got to watch as his path to stardom was paved.

However, my fascinations in even the sports my father enjoyed were vested in my own personal interests. Let me explain. Football was never of any interest to me—that is, until I became intent on becoming a cheerleader. When I tried out for a spot on the team, I was quickly informed that I had to have *knowledge* of the game in order to occupy a place on the team. Of course, that only made sense. We had to know whether to shout out "Defence! Defence!" or "Push ahead, push ahead, way ahead, way ahead!" The only thing to do was to get with the program. So off I went by my daddy's side to the Pontiac Silverdome, with season tickets to the Detroit Lions games, to learn the meaning of flags on the plays, field placement, player positions, etc. Now that wasn't as exciting, I must say, but to further my own cause, I pressed on. Fast forward to married life.

While one of my blending plights was learning the game of hockey and the dreaded game of golf, my husband had the daunting task of learning the ins and outs of shopping. Of course, that meant all shopping. Just as I had to adapt to all the sports that he enjoyed, he would have to become accustomed to the many facets of the shopping world. While he didn't particularly mind grocery shopping, he wasn't too thrilled with the idea of shopping for women's clothing or what he now affectionately calls "trinket shopping" for the purpose of home decorating—my absolute favourite hobby! He absolutely hated the idea of going to garage sales. I think it took him a little longer to get in line with my program than it did for me to conform to his, having been previously primed for his interests in my youth, having accompanied my father.

We found that not only were the things we once despised now of actual interest, but we also began to find sincere pleasure in them as well, not to mention the phenomenal bonding it produced in our marriage. I can tell you now that not only do I have my very own pink golf bag, complete with pink poodle covers for my woods, but I look forward to watching each tournament every Sunday afternoon after church, and I know most players by name. My point in it all is this: Yielding to each other's hobbies, interests, and desires not only helped us in becoming one, but it also became very beneficial in other ways as well.

Once while re-decorating our living room, I had the idea to have a scripture passage written on the main wall. The living room just happens to be my favourite room in the house, while my husband spends practically no time in that room at all. But when it came time to select the scripture, I really felt impressed to use my husband's favourite passage instead of my own. While all scripture is wonderful, my husband's favourite passage had not yet ever spoken to me as it had so deeply to him. Little did I know that the Lord would use that scripture to minister to me in the areas of our marriage where we were *not* bonding and in one accord. It is, in fact, the path to victory for the burdens not only of my heart, but of yours.

While many marriages can be basically pleasant or even happy in many or most areas, there can be hidden areas that are sources of great pain and/or despair. When my own personal pain was too much to bear, I reluctantly sought out spiritual counsel. I was told that I wouldn't like the answer I sought, but that it was, in fact, the answer for my situation.

"What about the pain?" I asked her. "How do I get healing for the pain?"

"When you help *him* to heal, *you* will be healed," she answered.

She was absolutely right; I didn't like the answer. This time, yielding to my husband meant caring more about his needs than my own pain, and it hardly seemed fair.

In the book of Joshua, we find written, "*Study this Book of Instruction continually. Meditate on it day and night so you will be sure to obey everything written in it. Only then will you prosper and succeed in all you do*" (Joshua 1:8, NLT). Just as I had needed to gain knowledge in order to achieve the things I desired as a young girl, it was now imperative that I learn and engage the strategies of the Lord for the healing and desired outcome I was seeking concerning my marriage.

The Apostle Paul writes in Philippians 2:4 that we are to look to the needs and interests of others, not only to our own. When we sow seed for the healing and restoration of our husbands in the area of his need, we open the way to reap the harvest of a healed heart and restored marriage. This brings us to the scripture written on our living room wall: *"You will keep him in perfect peace, Whose mind is stayed on You, Because he trusts in You."* (Isaiah 26:3). We can have peace in pursuing the plan of God while awaiting the desired results when we entrust our private pain to the Lord.

The key here is to trust in the Lord. In His awesome love, God gave me that which had so often encouraged my husband to now comfort me as I awaited His intervention and much-needed healing of my wounded emotions. You see, the chair in which I daily sat during my quiet time with the Lord is directly opposite the wall on which the scripture is written, placing it in ever-present view as a constant reminder of God's promise. What promise? you ask. The promise that He can be trusted. Instead of staying fixed on the problem, we can purpose to focus our attention on the needs and interests of another—in this case, our husbands. As we do, we pave the way to the victory and healing we've been seeking for ourselves. Again, we find wisdom from the Word: *"But seek first his kingdom and his righteousness, and all these things shall be yours as well"* (Matthew 6:33, RSV).

When we focus on what God is telling us to do, in the manner He tells us to do it, instead of using our own methods, He will see to it that all we ourselves are seeking will be added to us. And true to His character, it will exceed all that we have asked for or even thought possible (Ephesians 3:20). We never make a mistake in placing our trust in the Lord. We can know with confidence that He is both willing and able to handle the issues of our wounded hearts.

> *Let us hold tightly without wavering to the hope we affirm, for God can be trusted to keep his promise.* (Hebrews 10:23, NLT)

INTRODUCTION

When I first got saved, my favourite verse of scripture was Psalm 37:4: *"Delight yourself also in the Lord, and He shall give you the desires of your heart."* I still love that passage of scripture, but as the Lord began to grow me in His Word, I came to love another verse as my favourite: *"Wisdom is the principal thing; therefore get wisdom. And in all your getting, get understanding"* (Proverbs 4:7).

What brought me to first love Psalm 37:4 was the fact that if I loved the Lord and delighted in Him, He would give me the things my heart desired, which at the top of my list at that point in my life was a husband! I had been married twice before with disastrous results before surrendering my life to the Lord, but I was still willing to believe that happiness in marriage was attainable. I was a brand-new babe in the Lord and had no idea that God would get involved in my love life, let alone actually join me together with the perfect man for me and even oversee the process if I entrusted Him with the task. I was excited to know that the God of all creation loved me so much that what mattered to me, mattered to Him, and He was willing and able to handle all the particulars as I waited patiently for Him to arrange for its fulfillment. This time, God Himself was making the selection and handling all the details.

The Lord even provided the grace I needed for the three-year wait that was ahead of me, giving me His peace as I eagerly anticipated the unveiling of this wonderful gift He was preparing just for me. Fast forward twenty years, and seventeen years into the marriage of the desire of my heart for which I prayed. This brings us to the concept of the book you now hold in your hands and the experience of those first seventeen years that laid the foundation for the subject matter contained within these pages. As the saying goes, we teach best what we need most to learn. Throughout those first seventeen years, there was a lot of learning going on.

MY JOURNEY INTO WISDOM

When my husband, Dale, and I were married that spring-like day in late October, I was elated, to say the least. We'd had a short but very sweet courtship of two weeks before he proposed, followed by seven additional months of courting before we walked down the matrimonial aisle. I had prayed and sought the Lord diligently about the man of His selection for me, and I was absolutely positive that the man standing before me at the altar was the one.

My pastor, a wonderful man of God, well-respected in the community, and much loved, married us as family and friends watched as the fulfillment of the promise was sealed with a kiss. I was now Mrs. Dale Andrew Simmons. Praise the Lord! The oppression and depression of singleness had now ended, and I was entering the Promised Land of marital bliss … or so I thought. Don't get me wrong, I was blissfully happy, but we weren't yet entering the Promised Land. This, I think, is where so many of us miss it. We think that our exit from singleness is the entrance into the Promised Land, when it's only really the point of our next connection. This is where Proverbs 4:7 comes in. Let's look to scripture to gain further clarity: *"When Pharaoh finally let the people go, God did not lead them along the main road that runs through Philistine territory, even though that was the shortest route to the Promised Land"* (Exodus 13:17a, NLT).

THE EXIT IS NOT THE ENTRANCE

When the children of Israel were delivered from the hands of Pharaoh, they were free from the oppression of slavery, but those first few steps out of the land of Goshen weren't planted directly into the Land of Promise. In fact, they would have quite a trek ahead of them, and many obstacles before they would actually arrive in the Promised Land of Canaan. Such is often the case in marriage.

The moment we say "I do," we are joined together as husband and wife in the eyes of the Lord, but the state of perfection, or that continual state of harmonious bliss, hasn't yet been attained. It's a work in progress that is almost always accompanied by obstacles along the way. The obstacles we face can be many and varied and can place a strain on the relationship, causing it to snap under the pressure if we're not properly prepared for them. God took the children of Israel the long way around through the wilderness to the mountain of Sinai, knowing they were not yet ready for the battles they would face before entering the Land of Promise. The first order of business was not immediate occupation of the Promised Land but time set apart in worship of their God. This was their important next step, or "connection," before they would enter the land of Canaan.

When we say "I do," we've only just begun our journey into oneness, no matter how long or short the courtship. Nor have we learned everything there is to know about our spouse, like the little quirky things, and sometimes major flaws, that once went unnoticed when overshadowed by the glow of new-found love but now begin to surface. Unlike our heavenly Father, we all have flaws, we're not always trustworthy, and we make mistakes often—all things that make for some very bumpy roads of passage, to say the least. Some with a narrow escape, very nearly uprooting the newly, or even sometimes securely-established, planting of the marriage.

INTRODUCTION

The solid love we see in the lives of married couples who have celebrated thirty, forty, fifty years of marriage didn't happen overnight. Ask any of them and you'll likely hear that the way they made it through was by way of a wilderness. There were some valleys and some mountains, at least a few with rough terrain, but through commitment and an abundance of forgiveness, they were able to endure and enter their rest within the Land of Promise. None have made it through without at least a few rough patches and/or seasons of difficulty.

As the Lord began to birth this book in my spirit, He led me to the book of Exodus and the illustration of the children of Israel as the foundation for our journey to understanding the difficult issues we sometimes face in our marriages. Recognizing that it's a *process* is the first important step toward gaining clearer insight into what we might encounter en route to our happily ever after. We'll explore the stages of deliverance God brought the children of Israel through that led them from the place of suffering to the land of promised blessing and rest. Our first priority must be establishing God as the head of our lives as well as our marriages. The Bible tells us very plainly that without God, we can do nothing (John 15:5)! The first stop on our journey, then, must be making God our source for all things. In doing this, we secure the foundation that we'll need to endure the challenges we face on our journey into oneness.

> *"Therefore whoever hears these sayings of Mine, and does them, I will liken him to a wise man who built his house on the rock: and the rain descended, the floods came, and the winds blew and beat on that house; and it did not fall, for it was founded on the rock. But everyone who hears these sayings of Mine, and does not do them, will be like a foolish man who built his house on the sand: and the rain descended, the floods came, and the winds blew and beat on that house; and it fell. And great was its fall."* (Matthew 7:24–27)

Realizing our need for our Saviour within our marriages is the key that opens the door to the happy home of our dreams. *Keeping* Him at the centre of our marriages is the firm foundation that will ensure the weathering of any storms that come our way.

He alone knows the road ahead, and He alone can lead us through the wilderness times of life, ensuring our safe passage and arrival in the Land of Promise. James 1:5 tells us, "*If any of you lacks wisdom, let him ask of God, who gives to all liberally and without reproach, and it will be given to him.*" He goes on to tell us in verse 22 of the same chapter, "*But be doers of the word, and not hearers only, deceiving yourselves.*" Not only must we be willing to *hear* what God has to say in the matters of the heart and of life, but we must be equally as willing to heed and "do" that which He instructs us. When we follow the plan and direction of the Lord, we will find that even difficult terrain becomes more easily trekked when He is leading the way.

He led the children of Israel from the land of Egypt as a pillar of cloud by day and a pillar of fire by night. He led them to the waters of the Red Sea and not only parted those waters but also swallowed up their enemies within them. What looked like an insurmountable obstacle before them was used by God to deliver them and defeat their enemies. If we trust Him, God will guide us too through any difficulty we face, and He'll bring us safely through to the other side. Philippians 4:6 tells us, *"Be anxious for nothing, but in everything by prayer and supplication, with thanksgiving, let your requests be made known to God."*

At the close of each chapter are Scripture Confessions compiled from scripture texts used within the chapter. They focus on the topics and issues discussed and are written out as a prayer. When we seek God, thank Him, and come into agreement with His Word for our lives, we can see the answers to our prayers become reality. At the back of the book, you'll find additional Scripture Confessions for yourself, your husband, and your marriage. God has heard our cries and has come to bring us the deliverance we are seeking from Him, and, true to His character, He can do exceedingly abundantly above all that we have asked or even imagined (Ephesians 3:20).

Isaiah 61:1–3 explains:

"The Spirit of the Lord God is upon Me, because the Lord has anointed Me to preach good tidings to the poor;

> *He has sent Me to heal the brokenhearted, to proclaim liberty to the captives, and the opening of the prison to those who are bound; to proclaim the acceptable year of the Lord, and the day of vengeance of our God; to comfort all who mourn, to console those who mourn in Zion, to give them beauty for ashes, the oil of joy for mourning, the garment of praise for the spirit of heaviness; that they may be called trees of righteousness, the planting of the Lord, that He may be glorified."*

Our hearts may be aching from the heaviness of turmoil experienced within our homes, but God stands ready, willing, and able to restore the broken areas of our lives and marriages. He will heal our broken hearts, give us beauty for ashes, and replant what has been uprooted so that we have healed hearts and strong, firmly planted marriages that not only weather life's storms but stand the test of time, bringing glory to the Father. There is nothing too difficult for Him to handle. He is the Great I AM, and He still says to us today, "I will."

CHAPTER ONE

Restrained in Egypt

And the Lord said: "I have surely seen the oppression of My people who are in Egypt, and have heard their cry because of their taskmasters, for I know their sorrows." (Exodus 3:7)

The many years the children of Israel spent under the weight of oppression in Egypt serves as a good illustration of how we may feel in our marriages today, which have sometimes been years in turmoil. As I opened my Bible to the first chapter of Exodus, I was comforted within the first few verses as God showed me within them that His good plan for His children had not changed. Even though they were in a foreign land and in bondage at the hands of their enemy, God's plan for the children of Israel remained the same, and it remains the same for us today. We are to be fruitful, multiply, and exercise dominion and authority over the earth as His children and heirs of the promise (Genesis 1:28). Many of us, like the children of Israel, have been targeted by our adversary and are under attack. We too may be in a place where we are confused by the events that have occurred in our lives, distressed, and even bewildered by the pain of what's transpired.

The future we envisioned may be clouded by struggle and pain, but through it all, God still has His hand upon us, our peace and prosperity on His mind and in His plan, causing us to remain fruitful, regardless of our current difficulties. Also, like the children of Israel, we too may be truly grateful for God's keeping in the midst of the situation, but we're also eager to be delivered from it. Our hearts have been broken, and our dreams of happily ever after may have given way under the heavy weight of the war that's been raging. The heaviness of the oppression pushes us to a place of despair.

My husband and I experienced raging wars after only a very short time following our walk down the matrimonial aisle. I was thinking, *What is going on?* Difference of opinion, arguments over little things, arguments over big things, and all shortly following the months of courtship when we just couldn't stand to be apart, yearning for the day we could finally be together day in and day out. What a difference a day makes, and all because we have an enemy that doesn't like to see the plans and purposes of God succeed. He had put a wrench in our spokes, so to speak, and we began to wobble. I was still happy that I'd gotten married, but I wanted my happily ever after.

Gaining an awareness of some key tactics of our adversary can go a long way toward understanding the why behind the what of many of the adversities we face in our marriages and our lives in general. In John 10:10, Jesus says, *"The thief's purpose is to steal and kill and destroy. My purpose is to give them a rich and satisfying life"* (NLT). The enemy desires to oppose and hinder the working of the Lord in the lives of His children. Anything he can do to delay, postpone, or nullify God's purposes and plans for our lives is his intent. Oppression is a major weapon in his arsenal, used to thwart the fulfillment of God's good plans for His children.

According to the *Webster's Universal College Dictionary*, oppress means "to govern or manage with cruel or unjust impositions or restraints; exercise harsh authority or power over; 2. to lie heavily upon (the mind, a person, etc.) weigh down."[1] I was particularly struck by the phrases "to lie heavily upon" and "to weigh down." Although many of the issues we face within marriage are of a natural sort—such as finances and differences of opinion that can incite strife—what really plagues us is the heaviness of heart because of those issues, and the hurts those issues bring about. The natural circumstances are simply outward symptoms of deeper, inward issues—issues of the heart. We're admonished in Proverbs 4:23 to *"Keep your heart with all diligence, for out of it spring the issues of life."*

The enemy presses on our emotions, knowing their attachment to the heart. It's a clever ploy to attach our

---

[1] *Webster's Universal College Dictionary*, s.v. "Oppress," accessed December 12, 2021, https://archive.org/details/webstersuniversa0000unse_p5e0/page/n5/mode/2up.

feelings to our circumstance in hopes that we will act in accordance with what we see, feel, and/or *experience* in the circumstance, reacting from our emotions and speaking accordingly. He knows that reacting from the place of our bruised and wounded emotions will likely bring about unedited words and yield destruction. Proverbs 18:21 speaks to us, saying, "*Death and life are in the power of the tongue, and those who love it will eat its fruit.*"

Pressing on our hearts with the weight of troubles and difficulty is not only a common tactic used by our enemy, but it can also prove to be most effective, provoking us in our anguish to use our own mouths to set in motion untold harm (James 3:5). The enemy also uses the weapon of strife that springs forth from those very same pressed-upon emotions to set us up for failure and keep us from attaining the abundant life God has planned for us. Strife can virtually shut down the blessings of God in our lives and bring them to a standstill. Again, the aim of the enemy is to bring about strenuous opposition in efforts to impede our progress and keep us from experiencing the good life of milk and honey associated with Promised-Land living. What should be sweet like honey, he attempts to make sour and bitter. What should be abundance or abundant life, as milk is often referred to in Scripture, he strives to make into a life of hard bondage and difficulty rather than a source of happiness and fulfillment.

RESTRAINED BY OPPRESSION

And he said to his people, "Look, the people of the children of Israel are more and mightier than we; come, let us deal shrewdly with them, lest they multiply, and it happen, in the event of war, that they also join our enemies and fight against us, and so go up out of the land." Therefore they set taskmasters over them to afflict them with their burdens. And they built for Pharaoh supply cities, Pithom and Raamses. (Exodus 1:9–11)

In looking at this passage of Scripture, we find that the reason for the onslaught of oppression launched against the children of Israel by their oppressor, Pharaoh, King of Egypt, was due to his own insecurities. He feared being overtaken by those he believed to be superior to himself and his kingdom. He was afraid of those whom he sought to oppress. The fear of being overtaken and the possibility of losing the asset of skilled workmen vital to the continued success of his own kingdom's growth and prosperity was the motivation behind forcing them into the bondage of slavery and oppression. Although our adversary may not be afraid of *us*, he *is* afraid of the One Who resides within us. He's well aware of the authority we've been given and the mandate upon our lives.

The first portion of our scripture passage tells us that their multiplication was a threat to Pharaoh. Basically speaking, the intent was to devise a plan to stop the children of Israel from becoming more fruitful and to hinder them from prospering or advancing. We see, additionally, that he desired to keep them from fighting against *him*. Verse 10 reads, *"Come, let us deal shrewdly with them, lest they multiply, and it happen, in the event of war, that they also join our enemies and fight against us, and so go up out of the land."*

This is a major strategy of the enemy in our marriages. Instead of fighting him, he seeks to turn us against one another, doing his dirty work for him. He's also afraid of our escape from his realm of domineering influence, so he seeks to restrain us from the knowledge of the truth behind his attack and ultimately from taking the territory (Promised-Land living) that is rightfully ours.

Restrain means "To hold back; to hold from action, proceeding or advancing, either by physical or moral force, or by an interposing obstacle. To repress; to keep in awe; To suppress; to hinder or repress; To hinder from unlimited enjoyment; as, to restrain one of his pleasure or of his liberty. To limit; to confine."[2]

The enemy would like to keep us so immersed in oppressive circumstances and focused on our pain that the possibility of advancing and attaining the life of enjoyment God has planned for us seems impossible and/or unlikely, and so we succumb to the picture of a defeated life, composed by our enemy. Our hopes are so squashed that we allow the mud of affliction (or adverse circumstance) to obstruct our view of God's good plan

---

[2] *Webster's Dictionary 1828*, s.v. "Restrain," accessed December 21, 2023, https://webstersdictionary1828.com/Dictionary/Restrain.

and purposes for our lives, and we passively submit to a life less than intended and thus miss out on or forfeit our life of unlimited enjoyment.

Digging a little deeper, we see that the plan of the enemy not only brought destruction to the children of Israel at that particular point in time but, looking into the future, would also serve to defeat their own purposes as well: *"and he said, 'When you do the duties of a midwife for the Hebrew women, and see them on the birthstools, if it is a son, then you shall kill him; but if it is a daughter, then she shall live'"* (Exodus 1:16). In killing off the male population of the Israelites, Pharaoh would, in addition, reduce his own kingdom's future workforce, production, and increase as well.

Sometimes when the enemy plans an attack, the person chosen to administer said attack is unknowingly not only bringing destruction to another party but future destruction upon themselves as well, without realizing it. This is the case in many marriages when a spouse is being used to bring pain into the union. They fail to see the repercussions their actions will bring upon themselves as well as the others involved, such as their spouse, their children, and even family and friends. The enemy has them so focused on their own desires that they overlook the future implications of their actions. Pharaoh was so concerned about his own welfare and making provision for his own future success that he endangered his entire kingdom in the process.

When it comes to the marriage union, the kingdom at stake is the family. If your husband has been used as the instrument of destruction in your family, recognize that it's the enemy behind it. The devil knows that if he can take down the head of the family, the others will fall beneath him and so complete his mission to dissolve the entire family unit. Jesus says in Mark 3:25: *"And if a house is divided against itself, that house cannot stand."*

From the very beginning, God instituted the family to be the means by which He would bless mankind and fulfill His plan for the earth. At the heart of most every attempt on man's life is a link to the destruction of the family. Whether it's an addiction, such as gambling, street or prescription drugs, pornography, or any other addiction; infidelity; abandonment; or violent behaviour, it's been sent as an instrument to separate the heart of the husband from his family and cause their ultimate breakdown and dissolution. Whatever the method used to accomplish it, reduced increase and fruitfulness of the family unit is the intended result.

Another way in which the enemy cloaks himself and his work is by deceiving the hurting spouse. He attempts to deflect the onus from himself and cause us to see our spouse as the culprit, targeting them as the enemy. He pits us against each other so that we won't take authority over him, our true enemy, at his onslaught. The Bible shines light on this matter in Ephesians 6:12: *"For we are not fighting against flesh-and-blood enemies, but against evil rulers and authorities of the unseen world, against mighty powers in this dark world, and against evil spirits in the heavenly places"* (NLT). We need to redirect our focus onto the one who is behind the attack instead of on the one who is unknowingly being used to initiate it.

Remember that the enemy doesn't want us to be released from doing his dirty work. It was Pharaoh's fear that the children of Israel would *"go up out of the land"* (Exodus 1:10) that prompted his actions against them. The enemy seeks to use us as weapons against ourselves as we fight and attack one another and he cloaks himself, keeping us in the dark about his manoeuvres. Thanks be to God! He steps in and shines the light of truth into the dark places, allowing us to catch the thief and recover all.

In beginning the process of healing and restoration, we must see that we've been fighting the wrong battle if we've been approaching it through our flesh or attacking our spouse. We must get the understanding that our husband is not the enemy—Satan is the enemy. We must also see that it's going to take a mightier hand than our own to win this battle. If we've been waging this war in our own strength for any length of time, we need to abandon our way for a new battle plan, the plan of the Lord. God tells us in Philippians 1:28: *"Don't be intimidated in any way by your enemies. This will be a sign to them that they are going to be destroyed, but that you are going to be saved, even by God himself"* (NLT). No matter how difficult the battle, remember that even though the Egyptians hard pressed the children of Israel, they grew stronger in the face of it. It was the Egyptians that were in dread of the children of Israel, not the other way around: *But the more they afflicted them, the more they multiplied and grew. And they were in dread of the children of Israel"* (Exodus 1:12). Wipe the mud of affliction from your eyes; don't allow it to obscure your view. Get ready to see the salvation of the Lord!

SCRIPTURE CONFESSIONS

And the Lord said: "I have surely seen the oppression of My people who are in Egypt, and have heard their cry because of their taskmasters, for I know their sorrows." (Exodus 3:7)

Don't be intimidated in any way by your enemies. This will be a sign to them that they are going to be destroyed, but that you are going to be saved, even by God himself. (Philippians 1:28, NLT)

Dear Heavenly Father,

Thank You that You have seen all that's transpired in our marriage. Thank You that You know the heartache and sorrow it has caused, and that You hear my cry for help.

Thank You that I don't have to be intimidated by the situation, but that You are destroying the work of the enemy in our lives and in our marriage. Thank You for Your salvation. In Jesus' name, Amen.

Salvation: "The act of saving; preservation from destruction, danger, or great calamity. Deliverance from enemies; victory."[3]

---

[3] *Webster's Dictionary 1828*, s.v. "Salvation," accessed December 21, 2023, https://webstersdictionary1828.com/Dictionary/salvation.

CHAPTER TWO

I HAVE SEEN YOUR SORROW

And the LORD said, I have surely seen the affliction of my people which are in Egypt, and have heard their cry by reason of their taskmasters; for I know their sorrows; (Exodus 3:7, KJV).

AFFLICTION AND SORROWS

Affliction: "The cause of continued pain of body or mind, as sickness, losses, calamity, adversity, persecution. Many are the afflictions of the righteous. Ps. 34."[4]

Sorrow: "The uneasiness or pain of mind which is produced by the loss of any good. Or of frustrated hopes of good or expected loss of happiness."[5]

Going through distressing situations can be painful in and of itself, but the emotional anguish that sometimes accompanies the problem can bring about an inward suffering that is difficult to understand for those who have never experienced it, leaving one feeling alone in their pain and misunderstood. God assured

---

[4] *Webster's Dictionary 1828*, s.v. "Affliction," accessed December 21, 2023, https://webstersdictionary1828.com/Dictionary/affliction.

[5] *Webster's Dictionary 1828*, s.v. "Sorrow," accessed December 21, 2023, https://webstersdictionary1828.com/Dictionary/sorrow.

the children of Israel that He had not only seen their afflictions and distress, but He *knew* their sorrows. He was letting them know that He understood the heartache produced by the things they had suffered during their time in Egypt.

Egypt, also called "Mizraim," is often referenced as a place of bondage in the Bible. When I sought out its proper name definition, I found it to mean "two distresses" or "two-fold Egypt."[6] For our purposes, we can think of it as a combined distress, or the presence of more than one issue. "Two-fold Egypt" refers to upper and lower Egypt, or, for us, the concept of being all-encompassing. Satan would like to afflict us with such distress and difficulties that we feel encompassed by them on every side, but in 2 Corinthians 4:8–9, Paul encourages us by saying, *"We are troubled on every side, yet not distressed; we are perplexed, but not in despair; persecuted, but not forsaken; cast down, but not destroyed"* (KJV).

God reminds us that no matter the hardships, He won't allow our distress to destroy us. When troubles seem to surround us and we're perplexed and weighed down by our difficulties, we often desire to be consoled, comforted, and understood by someone close to us who will extend compassion toward us as we muddle through. We desire that someone "see" our sorrow. In the case of marriage, the one from whom we most often desire to receive such compassion is our husband.

---

[6] Alfred Jones, *Jones' Dictionary of Old Testament Proper Names* (Grand Rapids, MI: Kregel Incorporated, 1990).

SEE MY SORROWS

One of the things that posed a problem for Dale and I over the years was my desire for him to understand my feelings, especially when going through difficult situations or times of emotional strain. I sought understanding and compassion but often received terseness instead. I would explain to him why something had affected me so deeply. This would often be the case when it was something that I felt he had done or said that had occasioned the pain. When he couldn't understand the why behind the what, even after I'd so deeply and carefully explained it in detail, using many carefully placed and emphasized words, often accompanied by tears, I'd become angry. I viewed him as uncaring and became more upset with him, after trying to forcefully produce understanding, than I had been at the start. I hadn't yet learned to hold my peace and let the Lord fight my battles. I felt as if my tears and obvious discomfort meant nothing to my husband and was fuel to the already raging fire. More walls went up, producing a greater divide than at the onset.

What it boiled down to was anger on my part, stemming from an unmet expectation, which almost always produces anger leading to strife. Strife is another weapon used by our adversary to stifle our growth, fruitfulness, and productivity.

I've taught an anger management course at our church now for several years, and the Lord has taught me much on the subject. I laughed when the call came to teach it, but I happily accepted. Me, of all people, teaching anger management! Again, we teach best what we most need to learn. Not that I'm an angry person; I just needed to learn how to properly *respond* in my anger and was, and still am, a work in progress.

I have learned that there are four basic categories behind the why of our anger: unmet expectations, unrealistic expectations, unmet needs, and insecurity.[7] Usually, our anger can be attributed to one or a combination of these four categories. The key behind my anger toward my husband was the fact that I was expecting him to respond to me in a more loving manner, thus creating an unmet expectation. When he didn't, I became angry or upset with him. Why couldn't he understand my pain? The more I tried to make him understand, the worse the matter became.

Understand: "to perceive the meaning of; to be familiar with; have a thorough knowledge of; to grasp the significance or importance of; to perceive what is meant; comprehend."[8]

I wanted my husband to comprehend why the given situation had hurt me and then to respond with caring concern. When the person to whom we've come for support and/or comfort fails to respond in the manner we're expecting, offence is often the result. The question arises, "Why don't you care about how I feel?" Things

---

[7] *Overcoming Emotions that Destroy: Practical Help for Those Angry Feelings That Ruin Relationships*, Baker Books by Chip Ingram, and Becca Johnson, June 1, 2010.

[8] *Webster's Universal College Dictionary*, s.v. "Understand," accessed December 21, 2023, https://archive.org/details/webstersuniversa0000unse_p5e0/page/n5/mode/2up.

may begin to escalate with a verbal exchange, and a new can of worms is now open to combine with the original issue at hand. It isn't that we shouldn't share our feelings and concerns with our husband, or seek to obtain understanding, but when it becomes clear that they either have not, cannot, or choose not to understand our heart in the matter, forceful persuasion is not the answer.

My husband can tell you that I can say the same thing in about fifty different ways, but if he doesn't get it, the only change it will make is in his attitude. Pressing the issue only yields more disappointment, sorrow, and pain. Offence is a major tool of the enemy and gives him a foothold by which to produce further discord and distress in your situation. In Ephesians 4:26–27, the Apostle Paul tells us, *"And 'don't sin by letting anger control you.' Don't let the sun go down while you are still angry, for anger gives a foothold to the devil"* (NLT). The key here is not allowing your anger to control you, your words, and/or your actions. Doing so only opens the door for the enemy to wreak havoc. If you give the devil an inch, he'll gladly take a mile, adding insult to injury.

There is, however, One to Whom we can bring our pain, Who will not only understand but impart to us the wisdom necessary to bring about the healing and comfort we seek. Hebrews 2:18 states, *"Since he himself has gone through suffering and testing, he is able to help us when we are being tested"* (NLT). Not only will the Lord always be there for us to run to with our hurts, but He is also the One most qualified to minister to them. We're told in Isaiah 53:3a that "*He was despised and rejected—a man of sorrows, acquainted with deepest grief*" (NLT). Jesus understands our suffering and our sorrow. He *knows* how we're feeling. "Know" can be defined as: "to be acquainted or familiar with a thing, place, person; to understand from experience or practice."[9]

Whatever we have experienced, when we take it to the Lord, He will not only understand but is able also to identify with our pain as well. Jesus can say to us, "I know how long it's been going on. I saw where it started. I know how deeply it has affected you and the result of its effects."

I know that it's been difficult to bear. He bore the weight of the sins of the world on the cross of Calvary, so He can say, "I *know* your scars. I know how deep they are."

He was wounded for our transgressions (and the transgressions of others against us), and He comforts us, saying, "My wounds can heal your wounds." Not only does Jesus understand our sorrows, but He has also experienced them as well. Hebrews 4:15–16 teaches us:

> *For we do not have a High Priest who cannot sympathize with our weaknesses, but was in all points tempted as we are, yet without sin. Let us therefore come boldly to the throne of grace, that we may obtain mercy and find grace to help in time of need.*

---

[9] *Webster's Universal College Dictionary*, s.v. "Know," accessed December 21, 2023, https://archive.org/details/webstersuniversa0000unse_p5e0/page/n5/mode/2up.

The key to properly handling our sorrows and disappointments is found in the latter portion of that verse, as it tells us to come to God with our issues. Jesus is our great example for all things. This passage of scripture tells us that even when enduring great affliction, Jesus didn't sin. He didn't let anger or disappointment control Him, allowing it to bring forth sin. By the grace of God, we too can respond in like manner, keeping the door shut to additional access of the enemy into the situation.

My husband may not have been able to comprehend the magnitude of my sorrows, but my Lord understands. He has been there. As a matter of fact, He has already been in my tomorrows and knows the end of the matter and the victory that awaits me.

Instead of fanning the flames of strife by attempting to force understanding, we need to take our pain to the One Who will always understand. He will strengthen us as we wait for Him to bring about the change and healing we are seeking. In Matthew 11:28–29, Jesus says:

Come to me, all of you who are weary and carry heavy burdens, and I will give you rest. Take my yoke upon you. Let me teach you, because I am humble and gentle at heart, and you will find rest for your souls. (NLT)

God has seen your sorrow; He has heard your cry. He will give your weary soul (mind, will, and emotions) the much-needed rest you so earnestly desire. He will carry the weight of the burden and stay close by your side as He leads you gently through to the place of wholeness, fruitfulness, and blessing. Look up and wipe away your tears. Your deliverance draws nigh (Luke 21:28)!

The righteous cry out, and the Lord hears, and delivers them out of all their troubles. The Lord is near to those who have a broken heart, and saves such as have a contrite spirit. Many are the afflictions of the righteous, but the Lord delivers him out of them all. (Psalm 34:17–19)

SCRIPTURE CONFESSIONS

"We are troubled on every side, yet not distressed; we are perplexed, but not in despair; persecuted, but not forsaken; cast down, but not destroyed" (2 Corinthians 4:8–9, KJV).

"For we do not have a High Priest who cannot sympathize with our weaknesses, but was in all points tempted as we are, yet without sin. Let us therefore come boldly to the throne of grace, that we may obtain mercy and find grace to help in time of need" (Hebrews 4:15–16).

"Then Jesus said, 'Come to me, all of you who are weary and carry heavy burdens, and I will give you rest. Take my yoke upon you. Let me teach you, because I am humble and gentle at heart, and you will find rest for your souls'" (Matthew 11:28-29, NLT).

"The righteous cry out, and the Lord hears, and delivers them out of all their troubles. The Lord is near to those

who have a broken heart, and saves such as have a contrite spirit. Many are the afflictions of the righteous, but the LORD delivers him out of them all" (Psalm 34:17–19).

Dear Heavenly Father,

I thank You that when I am troubled on every side, distressed, and even perplexed by the situation, I have no need to lose heart or give up hope, for You are with me through it all. Thank You that You will not allow the weight of despair to destroy me. I give You the heaviness of this burden; please give me rest for my soul (mind, will, and emotions).

I come boldly to You asking for Your grace to be upon me. Please help me to learn of You and walk in Your ways. Thank You for being near and for Your deliverance from all that troubles me.

In Jesus' name, Amen.

CHAPTER THREE

I AM COME TO DELIVER YOU

And I am come down to deliver them out of the hand of the Egyptians, and to bring them up out of that land unto a good land and a large, unto a land flowing with milk and honey; (Exodus 3:8a, KJV).

UNSEEN INTERVENTION

One of the things that we sometimes struggle with is the inability to see the intervention of the Lord in progress. In the opening verses of Exodus 2, we see that God was already moving on behalf of His children as He goes about orchestrating the birth, protection, and strategic placement of their future deliverer in the face of a beautiful, new-born baby boy. He would later be drawn from the water and placed upon the path that would lead to God's deliverance for His people. His very name meant "drawn out," and not only would he be drawn from the threat of destruction, but he would later be used by God to draw his entire nation out from the destruction purposed for them by the Egyptians. Amid the children of Israel facing one of their most devastating hardships, God is skillfully arranging for their deliverance, right in their midst, unbeknownst to them.

The enemy is well aware of the destiny purposed for the children of God and desires to keep us in a place where we are not strong and oblivious to the presence and behind-the-scenes involvement of our loving God. He'd like us to believe that God has forgotten about us and our woes, but such is not the case. Even if the work being done at the moment is unknown and unseen by us, we can be confidently assured that no hurt or hardship suffered by a child of God ever escapes His watchful eye.

DO YOU SEE WHAT I SEE?

Moses had been born, but the children of Israel were not aware of his presence or the fact that he would be the one that God would use to bring about the deliverance they sought. The Bible tells us of his birth, rescue from death, and placement in the household of Pharaoh. Moses grew up right in their midst and learned of the workings of Egypt and of leadership, preparing him to fulfill his future destiny as the deliverer of the children of the Living God. Their deliverer walked right among them, yet none of these things were known by the children of Israel. But the process for their deliverance was well under way, nonetheless. Sometimes we don't see how God is working things out in our situations, but as His children, we can rest assured that if we're in need of help, God has seen it and has already developed a plan to bring about our deliverance from it, though at times in ways that may not be evident to us.

GOD WITH US

Moses is a type and shadow of our Lord and Saviour Jesus Christ. Jesus was born, saved from destruction at the hand of King Herod, and was raised and prepared for His destiny, all without the knowledge of most of all mankind. The Deliverer and Saviour of the world resided here and dwelt among us, but for most of His life, those He came to save were unaware of His presence among them. In our previous scripture verses, we have heard God say to the children of Israel, "I have seen your sorrow. I have heard your cry." Now He says to them, "*I am come down to deliver* [you]" (Exodus 3:8, KJV). In other words, I have come into the very midst of your situation. I am here.

The Bible tells us in Hebrews 11:1, "*Now faith is the substance of things hoped for, the evidence of things not seen.*" God may say something to us now, like "Believe that I have seen what you're going through. I have heard your cry, and I am working on your behalf, even if you don't understand how at the present moment. I have seen your sorrow. *Now see Me.* Believe Me. Be assured that I am with you even now, bringing about your deliverance and healing. Don't focus on what you still see going on around you, or what you can't see happening behind the scenes, but instead, focus on My promise. I will lead you out of your hardships and struggles and into the place of promise." As scripture tells us, *"Be still, and know that I am God!"* (Psalm 46:10a, NLT).

HOPE AND A FUTURE

Another area the enemy uses against us is in the area of past failures. Not only can we lose ground looking too far ahead, becoming discouraged by what we can't yet see, but we can also lose ground by looking back. As long as we're looking behind us, we can't make progress forward. As a matter of fact, looking back can sometimes cause us to wallow in bitterness and resentment. Lot's wife, in looking back, was turned into a pillar of salt (Genesis 19:26).

We too can choose to look back and remain focused on all the hurtful things our husband has said and done, as I had done so often in the past. We can keep an ongoing record of all his failures, repeatedly reminding him of the when and where, vividly recounting exactly how much he hurt us, or we can choose to let them go. The Bible tells us in 1 Corinthians 13:5–7 of how we are to respond in difficult circumstances by outlining the attributes of love:

> *It is not rude; it is not self-seeking, it is not provoked [nor overly sensitive and easily angered]; it does not take into account a wrong endured. It does not rejoice at injustice, but rejoices with the truth [when right and truth prevail]. Love bears all things [regardless of what comes], believes all things [looking for the best in each one], hopes all*

things [remaining steadfast during difficult times], endures all things [without weakening]. (AMP)

We say that we love our husbands, but when we look to the Word of God as it pertains to loving behaviour, we need to ask if we're showing love to our husbands in times of their shortfalls and failures, or only when they get everything right, saying and doing the things that make us happy. If the latter is true, we are not really loving our husband and are possibly in danger of developing a bitter heart toward him.

In the case of Lot's wife, looking back kept her from ever moving forward again. We too can make the same mistake and forfeit our future progress if we choose the path of bitterness, resentment, and unforgiveness, holding on to past failures. The only way to move forward is to leave the past behind. Forgive and forget and keep moving forward. The same holds true of our own failures. Sometimes we can blow it, know it, and not let go of it, holding on to personal guilt and shame.

We must draw a line in the sand and declare, "That was yesterday, last month, last year; this is a new day!" *"No, dear brothers and sisters, I have not achieved it, but I focus on this one thing: Forgetting the past and looking forward to what lies ahead"* (Philippians 3:13, NLT).

Sometimes it can be hard to forget what lies behind when it was laid at our doorstep only days, hours, or moments ago, and when the wound is still fresh. This is when we want to say, "But, God, you saw what he just did. You heard what he just said. How can I just simply forget about that?" God isn't asking us to act as if nothing happened, but instead, when it does, to bring that fresh wound to Him, allow Him to heal it, and keep believing Him for the change that is yet to come. That holds true for both you and your husband. God is able to bring change in us and our behaviour, just as He is able to bring change in our husband. We can release ourselves from past mistakes in the very same fashion as releasing our mate. We may not have achieved it yet, but we must choose not to dwell on the present circumstance. Doing so only keeps us from advancing ahead and is yet another trap of the enemy to keep us bound. The faster we let go of the offence, the sooner we can make progress in the right direction. Remember, nursing offences can keep you at a standstill. Don't let the sun go down on your anger. Don't give it time to fester. Don't give place to the devil, giving him room to advance instead of you.

When God sent His promise of deliverance, the children of Israel were, in fact, still in Egypt, but they had to decide that what God said, He would do, regardless of where they were at the present moment. Jeremiah 29:11 is a scripture of great hope and assurance, stating, *"For I know the thoughts that I think toward you, says the LORD, thoughts of peace and not of evil, to give you a future and a hope."*

The children of Israel were also in a period of captivity and struggle when the Lord spoke those words to them through the prophet Jeremiah, but He wanted them to see past where they were to where He wanted to take them, and He wants us to do the same. In other words, believe that He is working on our behalf by faith. By faith, believe His promise of deliverance. Let it become as substance to you. He brings us out of bondage to take us into the Promised Land! Not only *out*, but *in*. Not only *in*, but to a good and large land filled with abundance and sweetness.

The enemy would have us believe that our present circumstances are not only the now, but also the future. He'd also like us to believe that our past failures disqualify us from the possibility of attaining any hope for the future. In other words, don't hope. Don't dream. Don't believe. In the opening of Chapter One, I mentioned how comforted I was in the knowledge of God's keeping care as I began to write this book. Let me explain.

God showed me in the first verses of the scripture text, within the list of names of the sons of Israel that accompanied him to Egypt, that His plan for them had not changed, even though they found themselves in the midst of difficult circumstances. Sometimes when we come to long lists of names, often difficult to pronounce, we skip past them to the main portion of the text. In doing so, we can miss some very pertinent information.

In the first chapter of the book of Exodus, such a list appears, and it gives us the hope of which I am speaking. God showed me that every man and his entire household had come into the land of Goshen; not one was left out of His saving grace in providing for their protection and wellbeing from the famine and possible destruction. He had brought them there to keep them alive and to ensure their future posterity (Genesis 45:7). These were men who had sold their brother into slavery and lied to their father about it, causing him untold pain. Some had murdered innocent people in their anger over an injustice toward their sister. Still others had brought dishonour to their father in other ways. The point of the matter is this: regardless of past mistakes, God had not forgotten them, nor had He changed His mind about His good plans for them and their future.

Sometimes the difficulties we face are, in fact, the result of things we may have done in our past, although that's not always the case. They may come from a negative attitude we have held, bitterness, unforgiveness, resentment, or any number of things that have caused us to arrive at the place of difficulty we are facing, but God always has a way for us to escape the clutches of the enemy and get back on track.

Regardless of whether we ourselves have opened a door to the enemy through our own actions, or if it's simply an open attack of the enemy, God still stands ready, willing, and able to lead us out of the grip of the enemy and into the place of healing, peace, and fulfillment He has intended for us to enjoy as His children. If you find that you may have, in fact, contributed in part to some of the issues that you're facing, don't allow the enemy any further place in the situation by telling you that you don't deserve the intervention of the Lord.

No one *deserves* grace. No one *deserves* mercy; instead, it's given to us as a free gift from our loving God and Father, and there is no condemnation to those who are in Christ Jesus (Romans 8:1). We have all fallen short of the glory of God at some point in our lives. Confess and repent of any sin that comes to mind, seek the Lord for anything that He would have you do, and release yourself from any condemnation. First John 1:9 tells us that not only is God faithful to forgive us of our sins, but He also cleanses us from all unrighteousness when we confess them. God also sees the sorrow of a repentant heart. What a beautiful picture of the immeasurable love of God toward His children.

No matter how much damage has been done in the marriage, and regardless the source, God is still able to bring about the necessary changes to bring you to the place of healing and restoration. We may not always clearly see the road that leads to our deliverance, or even the path that leads to it, but God has already prepared the way. Our deliverance is already in motion regardless of the period of time in between. Leave behind the baggage of your past, the baggage of yesterday, or even of today. Even on the road to recovery, God has promised to make the time spent en route to the promise one that is paved, to lighten our journey and provide rivers of refreshing as we make our way through the dry places yet to be travelled. We can be assured that He won't only lead us from the place of sorrow and despair but bring us into the land of promise to enjoy the sweet life of milk and honey He has promised us.

> *"Do not remember the former things, nor consider the things of old. Behold, I will do a new thing, now it shall spring forth; shall you not know it? I will even make a road in the wilderness and rivers in the desert."* (Isaiah 43:18–19)

Don't give attention to how much has transpired in the past. Don't allow unseen progress to keep you in wonder. Be moved by *now* faith. Rise up and say, "Right now, God is moving on my behalf. Right now, He is straightening out the crooked paths and making them straight. Right now, it's springing forth. The process has already begun!"

SCRIPTURE CONFESSIONS

Now faith is the substance of things hoped for, the evidence of things not seen. (Hebrews 11:1, KJV)

No, dear brothers and sisters, I have not achieved it, but I focus on this one thing: Forgetting the past and looking forward to what lies ahead. (Philippians 3:13, NLT)

For I know the thoughts that I think toward you, says the Lord, thoughts of peace and not of evil, to give you a future and a hope. (Jeremiah 29:11)

"Be still, and know that I am God!" (Psalm 46:10a, NLT).

Dear Heavenly Father,

Please help me to continue in faith throughout this situation as You work things out for my good, even when things look contrary. Please help me to remain focused on You and Your Word instead of the circumstances around me.

Please help me to forget the pain of the past and let it go, even of yesterday or the previous moment. Please help me to forgive and forget past failures, both mine and those of my husband, and look instead to the good and wonderful plans that You have for us. Help me to be still in confident hope, knowing that You are God, and there is nothing impossible with You. In Jesus' name, Amen.

CHAPTER FOUR

I Will Send You

"Now therefore, behold, the cry of the children of Israel has come to Me, and I have also seen the oppression with which the Egyptians oppress them. Come now, therefore, and I will send you to Pharaoh that you may bring My people, the children of Israel, out of Egypt." (Exodus 3:9–10)

I WANT YOU

In the previous chapter, we talked about *now* faith and the right-now, ever-present intervention of our loving God on our behalf. In this chapter, we'll talk about now intervention from a slightly different perspective. We'll address *now* as it pertains to our personal involvement, and the role we ourselves are called to play in the process of our deliverance and restoration.

We say to God, "When will You come and bring about change?" God spoke to Moses when he asked much the same question concerning the children of Israel, and He responded by saying, *"Come now … I will send you"* (Exodus 3:10). God is the only One who can instill and ensure actual change, but He desires a willing vessel whom He can use as an instrument of change—someone He can work *through*.

PROTESTING THE PROCESS

Sometimes we seek change, but the change we desire is one to be made within someone else. We often kick against the pricks, so to speak, when we're asked to allow changes to be made within *us* before ever seeing evidence of progress in the one in whom we desire the changes be made—in this case, our husbands. We may find ourselves saying, as Moses once said, "Who am I?" We may even begin to protest the process. We don't always understand the path the Lord would have us take en route to the answer to our woes, so we begin to question the designated course.

In 2 Kings 5:9–14, we read the story of Naaman, a man very much in need of God's intervention in his own situation, who responded similarly.

> *So Naaman went with his horses and chariots and waited at the door of Elisha's house. But Elisha sent a messenger out to him with this message: "Go and wash yourself seven times in the Jordan River. Then your skin will be restored, and you will be healed of your leprosy."*
>
> *But Naaman became angry and stalked away. "I thought he would certainly come out to meet me!" he said. "I expected him to wave his hand over the leprosy and call on the name of the Lord his God and heal me! Aren't the rivers of Damascus, the Abana and the Pharpar, better than any of the rivers of Israel? Why shouldn't I wash*

in them and be healed?" So Naaman turned and went away in a rage.

But his officers tried to reason with him and said, "Sir, if the prophet had told you to do something very difficult, wouldn't you have done it? So you should certainly obey him when he says simply, 'Go and wash and be cured!'" So Naaman went down to the Jordan River and dipped himself seven times, as the man of God had instructed him. And his skin became as healthy as the skin of a young child, and he was healed! (NLT)

The number seven in scripture often represents completion. Dipping himself seven times in the waters represented complete compliance to the process he was asked to obey. We too will need to completely comply with all that the Lord requires of us in the process of our own healing and restoration. Naaman wanted the easy way out, wanting the prophet to simply wave his hand so he could be cleansed of his leprosy, but God had another plan.

We may ask, "Why not just do a work in my husband? Why do you need me?" Like Naaman, we too may be asked to get out of our comfort zone and take part in our own healing.

WHY ME?

I remember a time when a similar situation occurred in my marriage. As far as I was concerned, the problem we were dealing with rested squarely with my husband.

Just as I stated in the previous chapter, I was accustomed to making it known with each new circumstance, every detail of every offence. There finally came a day when I felt that the Lord wanted me to stop rehearsing details of former occurrences and simply address the issue at hand. Of course, this would mean lessening the impact of my message. The finally is only what just occurred; the matter of repeated offence is what made the point and declared my point so valid, to my way of thinking. How was I to win the war with only so small an arsenal? Nevertheless, I was sure about what I was being instructed to do, so I obeyed reluctantly.

At first, it was difficult. The more the matter seemed to slip toward non-compliance, the more I wanted to dig back into the past for more ammunition, but I tried to hold the line that I had been asked to draw. I didn't get it right at first, and it took many attempts *to* get it right, but eventually, there was success. Not success in winning the battle with my husband, but success in resisting the pull toward the past. There had been success in me. I had been changed. The Lord, by His grace, had brought change in my way of handling the situation, and I'm so very grateful.

I had to go at it time and again before finally coming to a place of full compliance. I'm not perfect, mind you, but as soon as I feel the Lord's gentle reminder as the words want to come forth, I, by His gentle grace, submit.

I had been asked to keep dipping into the water to be cleansed of my wrong behaviour, and completion came when there was complete compliance. Seven may mean seventy-seven, if that's how long it takes us to comply, but the outcome is worth it. I don't try to win the battles anymore, because I know that the Lord will fight for me and win *our* war.

If I win over my husband, I really haven't won at all. The victory is only really won when "we" win because we are one. When we cry out to the Lord about our marriages, very often it is us He will send, and it is *us* He will use to bring about the change we desire. We only hinder our own progress when we prolong or delay our obedience to the process.

YOU FIRST

We say that it's the "restoration" of our marriages we are seeking but, oftentimes, it's really *trans*formation that we are hoping for. We yearn for change within our husbands and their behaviour, but many times God will look to us first, to transform us and *our* behaviour, as the catalyst to facilitate the behavioural changes we seek in our men. The Bible tells us in 2 Corinthians 10:6, "*and being ready to punish all disobedience when your obedience is fulfilled.*" Basically speaking, the answer we're given is this: Yes, the healing you are seeking will come, and even all the issues will be dealt with, but you must be willing to be the one who yields to God's plan first.

A movie comes to mind just now, in which the Lord once taught me a very important lesson. I'm a huge John Wayne fan, and the illustration of which I'm speaking came via a film in which he played an ex-boxer who moved from the United States back to his native home of Ireland to retire from a life of fighting and settle down. Once there, he quickly fell in love with the redheaded beauty and woman of his dreams, played by the lovely Maureen O'Hara. Her red hair was outward evidence of the inward fiery temper and sharp-witted tongue of Mary Kate Danaher, the character she portrayed. After an exchange of words of love, a delayed courtship, and a wedding arranged by way of a bit of mischief, the two started down what would prove to be a turbulent road to oneness.

They embarked upon their first fight as man and wife in front of family members and guests at their wedding reception. Throughout the process she protested his authority, and he protested at her desires. That would be the crux of their whole problem. A broken bed, separate sleeping quarters, countless exchanges of snippy remarks, and a lively jaunt through the Irish countryside later, the matter would be resolved. When she finally submitted to his authority and he took notice of her needs, they were all at once at one with each other, and their happily ever after began … at the end of the movie.

We don't have to wait until the end of the line to enjoy the gift of marriage or begin our happily ever after.

We can experience the good land of milk and honey the Lord has promised right from the start, but in order to do so, we must first submit to God's plan. God says to the woman, "Respect your husband" and to the man, "Love your wife" (see Ephesians 5:22–29). We don't have to spend our first forty years wandering in a marital wilderness if we will get in alignment from the very beginning.

The problem in the movie came about because both parties wanted the other to be the first to do their part. She waited upon his love to be made evident in more than word, but also in deed, while he awaited the respect that he expected to be forthwith. If we will humble ourselves and are the first to submit to the will of God in the matter, we open the door for God to come in and begin the necessary work. As long as neither will comply, progress remains at a standstill, and husband and wife at a stalemate, leaving an open door to the enemy to widen the gap and further the divide.

THE ROAD TO CHANGE

God took Moses out of the place of his own self-sufficiency in Egypt and brought him to Midian, where He could further mold him into the man he was created to be. Leaving Egypt was only the first step in the next phase of his development. For Moses too, the exit from Egypt wouldn't represent his entrance into the fulfillment of his calling and destiny. There was still much to be done in his life to prepare him as leader and deliverer of God's people. In order for Moses to get to the point of his next connection, he had to first leave the place he was at. He had to leave all that had become familiar to him. He had to leave behind his old way of life. Oftentimes, in order for us to move forward, there will be things that we must first leave behind.

Much of what we may need to leave behind as wives may come in the form of abandoning our own stubbornness and controlling nature. We feel strong when we are in control and laying down the law: "Now hear this, I'm not going to take this anymore. I'm not going to sit still while you just do what you want to do. I'm not gonna do this, and I'm not gonna do that. *You're* not gonna do this, and you're not gonna do that." We feel strong when we're giving ultimatums and making demands for change, but if we're honest, we've had no real success with that particular method of attacking the situation. Attaining progress in our flesh is limited at best.

Moses fled from Egypt because he'd tried to get something accomplished in his own strength, having killed an Egyptian to achieve it (see Exodus 2:11–14). We too can bring death into our own situations if we persist in doing things in our own strength. Trying to force issues into change is much the same as Moses trying to force change for his brethren by killing the Egyptian. He had successfully killed *one* Egyptian, but still thousands more remained (Exodus 2:11–14). We may win a battle or two in our own strength, but we will certainly lose the war if we continue in our own strength. We can become so eager to bring about change and make headway that we go about it in all the wrong way. The Bible tells us in Romans 8:12–13:

> *Therefore, dear brothers and sisters, you have no obligation to do what your sinful nature urges you to do. For if you live by its dictates, you will die. But if through the power of the Spirit you put to death the deeds of your sinful nature, you will live* (NLT).

A change must be made in the way we approach things if we want to enjoy the kind of life we're seeking. We'll have to remain quiet when we'd rather retort with forceful opinion. We may have to be the first to say that we're sorry when we feel that we've done no wrong. We'll have to be willing to leave behind our old way of doing things for something new.

WHAT'S IN YOUR HAND?

When Moses stood before God at the burning bush, God used a portion of their time together to show Moses how he would be able to accomplish the great task he'd been given. Moses had protested at first, doubting that those to whom he was being sent would listen to him. He was thinking only in the natural and hadn't considered the most important aspect of his capacity for accomplishing the assignment set before him.

> *But Moses protested again, "What if they won't believe me or listen to me? What if they say, 'The Lord never appeared to you'?"*
>
> *Then the Lord asked him, "What is that in your hand?"*
>
> *"A shepherd's staff," Moses replied.*
>
> *"Throw it down on the ground," the Lord told him. So Moses threw down the staff, and it turned into a snake! Moses jumped back.*
>
> *Then the Lord told him, "Reach out and grab its tail." So Moses reached out and grabbed it, and it turned back into a shepherd's staff in his hand.* (Exodus 4:1–4, NLT)

In asking the question, "How will they believe me?" Moses showed that his thought was only on the task, not upon the One who was sending him to it. He had failed to see the most important aspect of the commission. He was being sent to the task, but it was *God* who would bring about all that He was asking of Moses.

When asked to throw down his staff, God was asking him to throw away all that represented his own ability and skill, the staff representing his capability and skill as a shepherd. When Moses threw the staff to the ground, it became a snake, showing that any ability apart from God, no matter how extensively trained, was not only a dangerous undertaking but would not yield the desired result. He was giving Moses the revelation, understanding, and confidence he would need to go forth to the task. His confidence would have to rest in God alone.

THE MIDIAN YEARS

Moses had learned much about delegation, authority, and leadership as a prince in Egypt, but in Midian he would learn the aspects of gentleness, compassion, and servanthood. His time spent in Egypt hadn't taught him all that he would need to fulfill his role as deliverer of God's people.

I think of the three years I waited for God to bring my husband into my life. Because of the graciousness of the Lord, He blessed me to know right from the beginning that He, in fact, had a husband for me.

I wasn't sure, however, how long I'd have to wait, but I spent the time reading books on marriage to become prepared. I read one book in particular several times over. After three years of reading and *re*-reading, I thought, *Surely now I'm ready!* Oh, how wrong I was. Knowledge is only one part of the equation; understanding is quite another. It's when we begin to *do* what we know that it really proves our measure of understanding of any matter. Our first year of marriage proved very clearly that I knew a lot but still needed very much to gain understanding of what I knew. I needed to learn how to *do* what I *knew*.

We sometimes become tired of waiting to see change in our husband and proceed to take matters into our own hands, so to speak, but our methods may leave much to be desired. Our husband has been given to us as a gift from the Lord and has been placed as the head of the household by the Lord Himself. We do ourselves a great disservice when we treat him disrespectfully. Even when they are, in fact, in error, the greater error is our own if we respond to them with disrespectful behaviour. We, like Moses, may have tried in our own strength and ability to bring about the deliverance we seek, but God says, "You're not ready yet. Come to Me and let Me teach you, *then* you will be ready."

WITHOUT A WORD

In the same way, you wives, be subject to your own husbands so that even if any of them are disobedient to the word, they may be won over without a word by the behavior of their wives, as they observe your pure and respectful behavior. (1 Peter 3:1–2, NASB)

In this passage of scripture, we as wives are the ones being addressed concerning our man's behaviour. The Lord addresses *our* response, not the issue of our husband's disobedience. The Lord is giving us the answers we need to address any such situation. The way to win the battle is to resist the urge to spout off, demanding change in combative argumentation, but instead display virtuous and respectful behaviour. *This* is God's battle plan.

We are reminded in Proverbs 15:1 that *"A gentle answer deflects anger, but harsh words make tempers flare"* (NLT).

Although the Lord is clear about His methods, He's not asking us to act as if our husband has done nothing wrong, or stating that we are to simply excuse his behaviour. What He *is* saying is that no amount of yelling, screaming, temper tantrums, or the like will move our husbands into appropriate behaviour. He's letting us know that proceeding with such behaviour will only serve to compound the matter. God quickly follows up the admonition to refrain from unbecoming behaviour with the appropriate plan of action: *You should clothe yourselves instead with the beauty that comes from within, the unfading beauty of a gentle and quiet spirit, which is so precious to God* (1 Peter 3:4, NLT).

I recently had a visit to the dentist's office for my regularly scheduled cleaning. This time, however, the results were far and away different from times gone by. My regular hygienist had recently moved away, and a new young woman was assigned to me. Where the previous hygienist had only used a simple hand-held tool to clean my teeth of plaque and debris, the new young woman used a motorized drill to do the same job. The result was teeth just as clean as they'd been previously, but in the middle of the night, I was awakened by a pounding and very painful headache caused by the earlier jarring of my teeth from the motorized tool. The somewhat older, more experienced hygienist had learned through knowledge, coupled with years of experience and training, that the gentle pressure of the appropriate tool would not only do the job correctly but also keep her patients from unnecessary pain later down the road.

Again, understanding knowledge attained was the key. The new young woman, just starting out, had learned the knowledge and steps of the process but lacked understanding of applying too much force. She had taken the easy way out by applying too much pressure to do a job requiring only a gentle application of the right sort. The easy way was to use force, but it yielded pain that interrupted both sleep and productivity well into the next few days. The better way may require more effort and a bit of extra training but will produce better results without added pain or distress.

The same is true in our marriages. Because we haven't been able to bring about change thus far, we might assume that increasing pressure is the only way it will come, but that is simply not the case. Galatians 6:1 tells us, *"Dear brothers and sisters, if another believer is overcome by some sin, you who are godly should gently and humbly help that person back onto the right path. And be careful not to fall into the same temptation yourself"* (NLT). Here, once again, we are instructed to apply gentleness as the means to attain restoration and peaceful resolve.

GIVE ME SOME TIME

In the book of Esther, we find the story of the beautiful young queen of the Persian Empire. She had been placed in that position after the removal of the former queen, Vashti, who refused to appear before the king at his request, resulting in her banishment. She had an opportunity to be an instrument of change but allowed her own personal desires, controlling nature, and negative attitude to guide her decisions, thus bringing her to a disastrous end.

Esther, however, having the same opportunity, chose a different path. Before she became queen, or could even be considered for this position of such great influence, she was subjected to a lengthy period of careful training. For twelve months she was ordered to submit to beauty treatments before being presented to the king. Scripture tells us that six of those months were dedicated to oil of myrrh, and an additional six months to perfumes and preparations for beautifying women (see Esther 2:12). She would have to be softened and fragranced before she would be presented to the king.

Sometimes we need a little smoothing out around the edges. We may need to add sweetness to the aroma of our mannerisms and conduct before we can present our case properly before our husband and receive the response we desire. Just as Pharaoh was the king in Egypt, and Xerxes the king and head of the Persian Empire, our husband has been placed in authority in our home, and it's to him that we are being sent to encourage positive change in the realm of our homes and of our family.

Just as Moses spent time in Midian in preparation to be sent to Pharaoh, and Esther spent twelve months with oil of myrrh and sweet perfumes, we too must be properly prepared to be effective. We might be talking, and our husband may in fact hear what we say, but without proper preparation and softening, he may choose not to listen. We must yield to whatever softening may be necessary to address our methods and approach so that our requests are received favourably by our husbands. Scripture tells us that even though Esther came to the king at an inconvenient time, she was received by him willingly, and he was open to her request. We too will have to follow the steps of the Lord's preparation for our personal softening and beautification if we want to be received with open arms by our husband.

We might say to the Lord, "Yes, but my husband hasn't listened to me in all this time, so why should he listen to me now?" The answer we may receive is to declare the Word of God instead of our own. Speak in *His* authority and not with forceful or controlling persuasion. It's the weapon of the Word in action that brings about the change.

As we close this chapter, I'd like to reiterate this one thing. As we look once again at our examples—Moses and Queen Esther, we're reminded that it wasn't the great education Moses received as prince in Egypt that made him ready for the Master's use, and it wasn't the beauty of Esther that paved the way to her placement as queen of an Empire, for she was beautiful before the treatments ever began, and Moses was intelligent and capable before his arrival in Midian. It was the process God took them through that made them ready to be used by Him. It wasn't until they submitted to the Master's process that they became the instrument of change they were called to be and were empowered to bring about the needed deliverance of their people. It's all about the manner in which we approach the situation and whether we choose to go in our own strength or in the Lord's.

If we will give up control and submit to the loving correction, instruction, and plan of the Lord, we too may hear God say, "Come, now; let's get started. I will send you."

"Now therefore, go, and I will be with your mouth and teach you what you shall say." (Exodus 4:12)

SCRIPTURE CONFESSIONS

Now therefore, behold, the cry of the children of Israel has come to Me, and I have also seen the oppression with which the Egyptians oppress them. Come now, therefore, and I will send you to Pharaoh that you may bring My people, the children of Israel, out of Egypt. (Exodus 3:9–10)

Therefore, dear brothers and sisters, you have no obligation to do what your sinful nature urges you to do. For if you live by its dictates, you will die. But if through the power of the Spirit you put to death the deeds of your sinful nature, you will live. (Romans 8:12–13, NLT)

In the same way, you wives, be subject to your own husbands so that even if any of them are disobedient to the word, they may be won over without a word by the behavior of their wives, as they observe your pure and respectful behavior. (1 Peter 3:1–2, NASB)

You should clothe yourselves instead with the beauty that comes from within, the unfading beauty of a gentle and quiet spirit, which is so precious to God. (1 Peter 3:4, NLT)

Dear Heavenly Father,

Thank You for choosing to use me in the process of bringing about change in my marriage. Help me not to yield to the sinful nature of the flesh but to yield instead to Your leading and direction. Please help me to properly submit to my husband and display the inward beauty that brings honour to Your name. Help me, Lord, to keep quiet when I would rather say things in spite, and to be respectful toward my husband in all things. Please clothe me with the unfading beauty of a gentle and quiet spirit.

In Jesus' name, Amen.

CHAPTER FIVE

Plagued with Opposition

Opposition: "1. Situation so as to front something else; a standing over against; as the opposition of two mountains or buildings. 2. the act of opposing; attempt to check, restrain or defeat. 3. Obstacle. 4. Resistance; as the opposition of enemies. Virtue will break through all opposition."[10]

Once Moses was released to embark on the task of delivering the children of Israel, they weren't immediately released from Egypt or their labours. God informed Moses ahead of time that it wouldn't be an easy or a quick process, but that they should anticipate opposition from their enemy. With their very first push to freedom, the children of Israel were not only stopped in their tracks, but additional labours, or *burdens*, were added to them as well.

> *That same day Pharaoh sent this order to the Egyptian slave drivers and the Israelite foremen: "Do not supply*

---

[10] *Webster's Dictionary 1812*, s.v. "Opposition," accessed December 21, 2023, https://webstersdictionary1828.com/Dictionary/opposition.

any more straw for making bricks. Make the people get it themselves! But still require them to make the same number of bricks as before. Don't reduce the quota. They are lazy. That's why they are crying out, 'Let us go and offer sacrifices to our God.' Load them down with more work. Make them sweat! That will teach them to listen to lies!"

So the slave drivers and foremen went out and told the people: "This is what Pharaoh says: I will not provide any more straw for you. Go and get it yourselves. Find it wherever you can. But you must produce just as many bricks as before!" So the people scattered throughout the land of Egypt in search of stubble to use as straw. (Exodus 5:6–12, NLT)

On the very first day the children of Israel attempted to escape the bonds of slavery, Pharaoh added to their labours, and the people were scattered. Instead of freeing them from their burdens, Pharaoh sent them deeper into the land of Egypt, searching in places they wouldn't have normally gone to seek what they needed for their work and survival. When so intensely stressed by the issues of life, we sometimes feel pressured to turn back to what the world has to offer to find the answers to our needs. We may venture into places we wouldn't ordinarily go in response to the pressures we are facing.

This, though, is a ploy of the enemy to drive us further into his realm of influence. Having held high hopes for change, expecting things to become better but instead having some new issue spring up in its stead, can sometimes drive us into a worrisome and bewildered state. This is not a new strategy in the arsenal of our adversary.

SLEEPLESS NIGHTS

The second of the ten plagues sent on the land of Egypt was frogs. Scripture tells us that there were so many of them, they filled both the kneading bowls and their beds.

> *So the river shall bring forth frogs abundantly, which shall go up and come into your house, into your bedroom, on your bed, into the houses of your servants, on your people, into your ovens, and into your kneading bowls. And the frogs shall come up on you, on your people, and on all your servants.* (Exodus 8:3–4)

The presence of the frogs in the kneading bowls and on their beds would make it difficult to prepare meals or sleep comfortably, or even at all. The fact that they would affect Pharaoh as well as the people and all his servants would liken the severity of it to have affected the heads of all the households, all other members of the households, as well as those who served the households in any manner. What comes to mind for us today is the stress of mind that accompanies the presence of numerous trials, touching both us and those we love and are closest to. We become so focused on those issues that it becomes difficult for us to eat or sleep due to our worry over them. Worry is another major tool of the enemy.

Worry: "1. To tease; to trouble; to harass with importunity, or with care and anxiety. Worry him out till he gives his consent. 2. to fatigue; to harass with labor; 3. To harass by pursuit and barking; as, dogs worry sheep."[11]

When the enemy attempts to *worry* us, there are any number of methods he may employ. It may come in the form of a job layoff, a wayward child, various financial issues, a child skipping or dropping out of school, breakdown of the family vehicle, or a necessary major household repair. The matter can be worsened by the interaction of husband and wife over the matter, when varying opinions are held, making the effects yet that much farther reaching. Whatever the case may be, the goal is to harass us with the labour of dealing with worrisome issues to the point of becoming overwhelmed or pushed to our limits, thus driving us over the edge.

I'd like to focus for a moment on the portion of the definition that states, "to harass by pursuit and barking; as, dogs worry sheep." A few days after reading this definition, I watched a movie I had purchased, not knowing anything about it, having only read the storyline on the back cover, as being a sweeping British love story set in the countryside of England. In it, a young man had recently purchased two hundred head of sheep, desiring to become a sheep farmer. He owned two sheep dogs, one that was well trained and compliant, and another that was difficult to train, resistant, and even defiant. One evening after the farmer had gone to sleep after a

---

[11] *Webster's Dictionary 1828*, s.v. "Worry," accessed December 21, 2023, https://webstersdictionary1828.com/Dictionary/worry.

long day's work, he was awakened by the whimpering of the well-trained dog, which was lying at his side on the floor nearby. When he awoke, he heard the noise of the bleating of the sheep he had placed in the pen for safekeeping through the night.

He rose to his feet to find that the unruly dog had gone out in the night into the pen and *worried* the sheep, causing them to break away from the pen, driving them through the countryside and over a cliff, where they plunged to their death. I was amazed as I watched the definition play out before me in the scenes of the movie. The analogy? The enemy seeks to drive us with worries from the place where our Good Shepherd has purposed for our safety and protection, forcing us to scatter in directions that are harmful and even deadly, if possible.

THE GOOD SHEPHERD

A scriptural example of this very thing comes to mind just now. In 1 Samuel 1, we read the story of Hannah, a woman who endured issues of infertility in the beginning of her marriage and was taunted by her husband's second wife.

> *Now there was a certain man of Ramathaim Zophim, of the mountains of Ephraim, and his name was Elkanah the son of Jeroham, the son of Elihu, the son of Tohu, the son of Zuph, an Ephraimite. And he had two wives: the name of one was Hannah, and the name of the other Peninnah. Peninnah had children, but Hannah had no children. This man went up from his city yearly to*

worship and sacrifice to the Lord of hosts in Shiloh. Also the two sons of Eli, Hophni and Phinehas, the priests of the Lord, were there. And whenever the time came for Elkanah to make an offering, he would give portions to Peninnah his wife and to all her sons and daughters. But to Hannah he would give a double portion, for he loved Hannah, although the Lord had closed her womb. And her rival also provoked her severely, to make her miserable, because the Lord had closed her womb. So it was, year by year, when she went up to the house of the Lord, that she provoked her; therefore she wept and did not eat. (1 Samuel 1:1–7)

The first portion of our definition for the word "worry" was "to tease." Hannah endured such teasing that it drove her to a state of worry, which caused her to stop eating, something, I might add, that we need for the sustenance of our natural life. Worry can lead us, if allowed, to deeper issues that would seek to take more than the issue at hand. When we focus so much on the problem, it's easy to lose sight of the blessing that is still before us in the face of our husbands. The enemy would have us so distracted by the pain of the problem that we fail to focus on or give attention to our husband, leaving the door wide open to drive *him* away. The following verse helps to give us more clarity, and needful warning: "*'Why are you crying, Hannah?' Elkanah would ask. 'Why aren't you eating? Why be downhearted just because you have no children? You have me—isn't that better than having ten sons?'*"

(1 Samuel 1:8, NLT). Hannah's husband points out a very important factor in that even though Hannah had no sons, she still had him, and he was very good to her, better than *ten* sons. You see, we must be careful not to forget about our husbands in the midst of our pain. Doing so can make them feel neglected, and even as if they are not a necessary or important part of our lives, being so entirely focused on the pain.

My husband and I have a blended family—a son and a daughter from his previous marriage, and our youngest, a son from my previous marriage. When we married, I was convinced that we would have children together and build upon our family. We both shared that desire and dream equally. We thought we would add *two* additions—a boy and a girl. We felt so strongly about their arrival that we named them by faith and called them by name whenever we talked on the subject. Their names were to be Nina and Asa. Several years of waiting later, our dream was squashed by an unexpected trip to the hospital and an emergency hysterectomy a few days later. I was devastated, to say the very least. I had gone so far as to have reserved one of the rooms in our house for our new additions, which was painted over by a close family friend while I recovered in the adjacent room following the surgery. I went into a deep depression, and continual crying was nearly a way of life throughout the several months of recovery.

Although my husband never threatened to leave, he *was* upset about my extended expression and disappointment over our loss. My tears were my focus each day, not him. He's not a selfish man by a long shot, and he stood by my side all the way through the process, but he wasn't going to allow me to ruin our tomorrows by staying focused on the loss of yesterday, great though it was. He made it plain one day when he told me to stop mourning our loss and look ahead to the other things God has in store for our future. What a wakeup call. You see, the enemy would like to harass us over our issues so much that our attention is fixated on the hardship instead of on our husbands and the other blessings before us, opening the door for the issues to drive a wedge and tear us apart, leaving us with nothing at all.

When we go through one of life's valleys, we need to remember to keep our eyes on the Good Shepherd, who will lead us beside still waters as we recover and onward, all the way through the things that would try to overshadow our tomorrows. We don't have to fear, for the Lord is with us and will both comfort us and lead us through to brighter days. Our three children are a huge blessing to us, and we're a very happy family unit. God has since added two "grand" children to us—a boy and a girl—and we love them both dearly. God is so very good.

First Peter 4:12 tells us, *"Dear friends, don't be surprised at the fiery trials you are going through, as if something strange were happening to you"* (NLT). When opposition and hardships arise, we shouldn't be surprised by them, nor are we to be moved by them, but instead we should recognize them as the trick of the enemy that they are. We are to stand our ground, knowing that the outcome will be established by the Lord on our behalf. Just as Pharaoh was unwilling to obey God's command to let His people go, the devil is never ready to comply with the will of the Lord, so he seeks to keep us bound in whatever way he can, be it sorrow, loss, or problematic issues. If he can't trip us up one way, he'll attempt another. Our goal is to stand strong through the tests, trials, struggles, and obstacles as they come, while the Lord battles the enemy on our behalf. This, however, isn't always *easy* but is always possible through the power and strength of the Lord: *"For I can do everything through Christ, who gives me strength"* (Philippians 4:13, NLT).

The enemy sought to hinder the release of God's people by added pressures and worrisome troubles and burdens, but God immediately stepped in to deal with the hardness of Pharaoh's heart. It was this hardness of heart that prompted the plagues to bring about his compliance to the will of God for His people. This, though, created a period of delay in their release and slowed the progress in the process of their deliverance.

A HOLDING PATTERN

Holding Pattern: "a traffic course held by aircraft at specified location until cleared for landing; a condition of no progress or change."[12]

---

[12] *Webster's Universal College Dictionary*, s.v. "Holding Pattern" (New York, NY: Random House, 2010).

Moses had been sent to the children of Israel by the Lord to free them from their bondage, yet their release remained delayed for a lengthy period of time. I think of an airplane beginning its descent in anticipation of its landing but having to instead maintain a circling pattern for an undetermined period of time. We often feel as if we're going around in circles as we await the deliverance we seek, and it seems that we're not gaining any ground or making any progress. Just as God placed stumbling blocks in the way of Pharaoh due to his hardness of heart, He will thwart the opposition of our enemy in his attempts to hinder our release and deliverance. We will have to remain patient throughout the process, as God may address specific issues within your husband and soften possible areas of hardness in his heart.

STUBBORNNESS OF HEART

Stubborn: "1. Unreasonably obstinate; inflexibly fixed in opinion; not to be moved or persuaded by reasons; inflexible; 2. Stiff; not flexible."[13]

Our husbands may become hardened toward us and our desires because of issues that have become major points of contention between the two of you over time. He may become unreasonable, obstinate, carry an inflexible opinion, and not be moved or persuaded by our reasoning. Not to make light of more serious issues that you may face in this area, I just want to make a point

---

[13] *Webster's Dictionary 1828*, s.v. "Stubborn," accessed December 21, 2023, https://webstersdictionary1828.com/Dictionary/stubborn.

concerning a time when my husband remained inflexible for several years. God has given us a lovely home, and as I have stated before, my absolute favourite hobby is decorating.

We have an older home and have lived there since our wedding. The previous owners did make some upgrades before we purchased the home, even changing out the kitchen cupboards for what was—and I stress, *was*—a beautiful upgrade to honey oak cabinetry, my absolute least favourite colour of stain. However, they're solid wood and sturdy. I simply couldn't stand their colour.

I asked my husband time and again if we could paint them. Each time the answer was, "No, you just don't paint over nice wood." Ugh! He was truly inflexible and wouldn't move in his opinion. This went on from time to time for more than fifteen years! Finally, he gave in.

A good friend of ours owns a painting company and was willing to not only do the job but submitted a more than reasonable quote, desiring to simply bless us in getting it done. They turned out beautiful! And guess what—my husband loves it just as much as I do. Long overdue, and we circled round about the matter for many a day, but we finally came in for a happy landing on the issue, and we both are enjoying the change. I thank God that He gave me the grace to wait it out. It may have never happened had I filled the air with continual nagging and bitter complaint. The Song of Solomon 2:15 tells us that it's the little foxes that spoil the vine. Sometimes small though they may be, we can allow issues of insignificance to mount up into big issues that divide and separate. We are reminded in scripture that it's soft (not harsh) words that turn away wrath (Proverbs 15:1).

God is able to soften the heart of your husband. Scripture tells us that *"The king's heart is in the hand of the LORD"* (Proverbs 21:1a). We may not know how to reach them, but the Lord knows, loves, and is concerned for both you and your husband, and He desires that healing and restoration be enjoyed by you both, individually and as husband and wife. No matter how many issues have come to oppose the way of progress, no matter how hard your husband's heart may have become, no matter how long you've been in a holding pattern, God is able to cause the enemy to relinquish his hold.

PURSUED IN THE DESERT

Once the children of Israel had finally made it through the time of opposition, trial, and delay throughout the duration of the plagues in Egypt, they were free to leave its confines. But no sooner had they begun to make headway than they were once again pursued by their enemy, who was angered by their departure. The enemy is never happy when we're living free. Pharaoh mounted a task force in pursuit of God's people, chasing behind them, armed and ready for battle. As if all that he had done previously wasn't enough, he now sought to bring them back to the place of bondage from which they'd just broken free.

There may be times when you feel as if you've finally made a measure of progress and are on your way to definite change, but no sooner do you get over one hurdle when another is chasing at your heels. You see one more problem approaching and wonder if retreating is the answer, but retreat is not an option. God brought you out to take you in. Although the children of Israel were pursued by the enemy once they departed Egypt, God barred their way from harming them ever again.

The Bible tells us in Isaiah 59:19:

So shall they fear the name of the Lord from the west, and His glory from the rising of the sun; when the enemy comes in like a flood, the Spirit of the Lord will lift up a standard against him.

Right in the midst of the enemy's charge, God raised up a pillar of cloud by day and a pillar of fire by night to bar their way from touching the children of Israel or advancing any further. Although the situation appeared dire as they looked back and saw the pursuing chariots behind them, and the Red Sea before them, they were unknowingly on the very brink of their deliverance.

Then the Lord gave these instructions to Moses: "Order the Israelites to turn back and camp by Pi-hahiroth between Migdol and the sea. Camp there along the shore, across from Baal-zephon. Then Pharaoh will think, 'The Israelites are confused. They are trapped in the wilderness!' And once again I will harden Pharaoh's heart, and he will chase after you. I have planned this in order to display my glory through Pharaoh and his whole army. After this the Egyptians will know that I am the Lord!" So the Israelites camped there as they were told. (Exodus 14:1–4, NLT)

Sometimes when we face what appears to be impending factors that will worsen an already difficult situation, we need to camp out at a place where our own efforts are futile to allow the Lord room in our situation to go to work on our behalf. We will have to get out of the way, so to speak. This may mean refusing to harp on a given situation but instead remaining quiet on the subject. It may mean that even though you're not at all comfortable with a particular issue, you stay put, not attempting any advancement whatsoever but allowing the Lord to take the lead. If we will step aside, God is able to both bring about our deliverance and defeat our enemies all in the same action.

AND THE WATERS PARTED

But Moses told the people, "Don't be afraid. Just stand still and watch the Lord rescue you today. The Egyptians you see today will never be seen again. The Lord himself will fight for you. Just stay calm." (Exodus 14:13–14, NLT)

The final delay for the children of Israel before finding relief from their Egyptian enemy was the Red Sea.

Having camped out through what must have been a very difficult night of fear, anxiety, and worry, they were amazed to find that the water that had barred their way was now being parted. All through the night God parted the sea to open the way for their escape to freedom, giving them passage through the waters on dry ground. This is a picture of what the Lord will do for us if we will rest from our efforts and yield way for Him to act on our behalf. He will remove any and all hindrance, no matter the size, that would stand in the way of our freedom and deliverance.

> *When all the Israelites had reached the other side, the Lord said to Moses, "Raise your hand over the sea again. Then the waters will rush back and cover the Egyptians and their chariots and charioteers." So as the sun began to rise, Moses raised his hand over the sea, and the water rushed back into its usual place. The Egyptians tried to escape, but the Lord swept them into the sea. Then the waters returned and covered all the chariots and charioteers—the entire army of Pharaoh. Of all the Egyptians who had chased the Israelites into the sea, not a single one survived.* (Exodus 14:26–28, NLT)

What should have been an impenetrable obstacle to swallow them up in utter defeat, God made to be the highway to their freedom instead. They walked right through on dry ground with nothing to drag them down or impede their progress, every obstacle removed, and every enemy defeated. The Bible tells us in Psalm 30:5b, "*Weeping may last through the night, but joy comes with the morning*" (NLT). They had endured a night of turmoil, but with the light of dawn, God swallowed up their enemy right before their eyes, never to be seen again.

As you wade through the difficulties of life, be reminded that the great I AM is acting on your behalf and will do whatever is necessary to bring you out from the things that would trouble you, worry you, or attempt to stand in the way of your progress. The plagues of Egypt were a demonstration of God's power and involvement on behalf of His people, defending them and addressing the issues that opposed them. God will bring you out with a mighty hand, part the waters that would block your way to freedom, and swallow up all of your enemies within those very same waters. In the midst of your most difficult trials and struggles, be reminded of the children of Israel as they stood on the brink of disaster as the waves of the Red Sea stood in their way to deliverance. Remember who goes before you. Sing unto the Lord a new song. Stand in awe at His mighty wonders. If God be for you, who can stand against you?

> *Then Moses and the people of Israel sang this song to the L*ORD*: "I will sing to the Lord, for he has triumphed gloriously; he has hurled both horse and rider into the sea. The Lord is my strength and my song; he has given me victory. This is my God, and I will praise him—my*

father's God, and I will exalt him! (Exodus 15:1–2, NLT)

SCRIPTURE CONFESSIONS

The king's heart is in the hand of the Lord, like the rivers of water; He turns it wherever He wishes. (Proverbs 21:1)

It does not rejoice about injustice but rejoices whenever the truth wins out. Love never gives up, never loses faith, is always hopeful, and endures through every circumstance. (1 Corinthians 13:6–7, NLT)

So shall they fear the name of the Lord from the west, and His glory from the rising of the sun; when the enemy comes in like a flood, the Spirit of the Lord will lift up a standard against him. (Isaiah 59:19)

Father God in Heaven,

I thank You that my husband's heart is in Your hands and for making the necessary changes within him. Please help me not to rejoice in pride that he is being corrected but rejoice only that You are making us whole.

Please help me to love him unconditionally through the process of our restoration, without giving up on him or on our marriage. Please give me the faith to remain hopeful under all circumstances. Thank You, Lord, that when the enemy comes in like a flood, You raise up a standard against him on our behalf.

In Jesus' name, Amen.

CHAPTER SIX

THE DESERT SEASON

During the plagues in Egypt, God dealt with the resistance of Pharaoh, addressing the problematic attitudes and behaviours of others toward the children of Israel. For us, that may mean God beginning a work in our husbands to address some issue or trait that may have presented an area of conflict, or issues of turmoil within our marriage.

We need to realize, though, that exposing some area of needed correction or negativity within our husbands is only a part of the equation. The Lord will also need to expose any harmful, unbecoming behavioural traits within us for light to truly permeate the situation and bring about the changes we so deeply desire. Not only does God desire us to display a gentle and quiet spirit as He completes the required work within our husbands, but yielding to Him for the necessary work to be done within *us* will also be required. We will have to allow Him to address any areas of hostility, underlying bitterness, or resentment that may be festering beneath the surface of our own heart. In the wilderness, it was not the issues of *others* that God dealt with but with the children of Israel and their own personal issues and areas of concern. Now comes the time for God to speak to us as wives and the uglies that may be hiding within us that may have contributed to our time spent wandering around in the wilderness for so long.

IT'S ALL ABOUT ME

Attitude: "Feeling or way of thinking that affects a person's behavior."[14]

One of the main reasons the children of Israel remained in the desert for so long was the issue of attitude. They murmured and complained almost constantly from the time God began to deliver them from Egypt, during their departure and deliverance from it, and up to and including their arrival and stay in the wilderness. Our attitude plays a large part in how long we stay in the desert season(s) of our lives. The attitude we carry concerning our husbands and their behaviour may be a major contributing factor in the length of time we have already spent in our current dry season thus far.

---

[14] *Webster's Canadian Dictionary & Thesaurus*, s.v. "Attitude," accessed December 21, 2023, https://archive.org/details/websterscanadian0000unse/page/n5/mode/2up.

Remember our Scripture reference from a few chapters back? After our obedience is first fulfilled? Matthew 7:3–5 expands on this, saying,

> *"And why worry about a speck in your friend's eye when you have a log in your own? How can you think of saying to your friend, 'Let me help you get rid of that speck in your eye,' when you can't see past the log in your own eye? Hypocrite! First get rid of the log in your own eye; then you will see well enough to deal with the speck in your friend's eye."* (Matthew 7:3-5, NLT)

Now comes the time for God to address *our* attitude, *our* issues, *our* disposition, and *our* unbecoming behavior.

We're often so concentrated on the flaws of our husbands that we fail to see the even more important flaws within ourselves. We will need to submit to the Lord and allow Him to remove any log of obstruction in our own lives that would be a hindrance or obstacle in our marriage.

There is sometimes the need for an attitude adjustment in our lives, and the wilderness is the place where it's often addressed. Our attitude can tell a lot about the inward issues of our hearts. Attitudes are an outward expression of our inward thoughts, emotions, and feelings. They can vividly display, by our tone of voice and/or coldness or rudeness of behaviour, that we may still carry unresolved hurts or wounds from past offences. Our body language can also demonstrate negative attitudes and display offensive and disrespectful behaviour. A sour attitude may suggest that resentment is present beneath the surface and be made apparent by way of a spiteful attitude or prideful smugness carried toward our husband. It may be especially present when dealing with areas of repeated or recurring offense.

PEACE OUT

For me, I simply got to a place where I just didn't want to deal anymore. I would get so tired of the struggle that I would simply disengage entirely. Keeping our hands off a matter for the Lord to handle and shutting down to the process are two different things entirely, and it's all about our attitude.

Being peacefully, sweetly submissive and allowing the Lord to work isn't the same as being deliberately distant, defiant, and consumed with self-pity. Remember that the Lord needs us to be a willing, active participant in the process of our own healing. We need to be *all in* and fully engaged. Sometimes when we've been hurt to the core time and again, we simply don't want to try anymore, so we resort to what is often referred to as the silent treatment or the cold shoulder. We withhold our attention or affections. We stop making dinner, making him fend for himself. Or my former personal favourite, we simply pout. He can "see" what I won't say. Even though we're not saying anything with actual words, the absence of those words is saying a great deal. We are making it plain that we are angry. We are saying very clearly that we are punishing our husbands because of their actions toward us. We're attempting to make them drink bitter water by withholding any semblance of a sweet disposition.

THE WATERS OF MARAH

Upon their exit from the Red Sea, the first place the children of Israel came to was a place called "Marah," so named for the bitterness of the water drawn from the wells there. Sometimes the attitudes we carry are so acrid that it becomes evident we are drawing from wells tainted with bitterness and resentment of pains gone by, which we have not yet allowed the Lord to heal.

Bitter: "Sharp or biting to the taste; acrid; like wormwood; cruel; severe; sharp, as words, reproachful; sarcastic; sharp to the feeling; piercing; painful; as a bitter cold day, or a bitter blast; painful to the mind; calamitous; hurtful; very sinful."[15]

If our current behaviour displays any of these characteristics, we can see, by definition, that not only is it sinful, but that bitterness may still be present in our heart. Are your words sharp? Do they bite, belittle, or tear down? Are you sarcastic, vindictive, unkind, or callous toward your husband? We can't allow our pain to turn us into a bitter, sharp-tongued, and disagreeable woman, disrespecting and demeaning the gift of our husbands, no matter how difficult the issues we're experiencing may be. When we are berating, we are

---

[15] *Webster's Dictionary 1828*, s.v. "Bitter," accessed December 21, 2023, https://webstersdictionary1828.com/Dictionary/bitter.

simply wrong, no matter how right we are about the behaviour or circumstance being addressed. Hebrews 12:15b cautions us to *"Watch out that no poisonous root of bitterness grows up to trouble you"* (**NLT**).

The poison of bitterness works against us, not for us, and can bring added misery into our situation if we continue in it. We are the ones to become the target of troublesome worries when we yield to bitterness, not our husbands: *"Looking diligently lest any man fail of the grace of God; lest any root of bitterness springing up trouble you, and thereby many be defiled"* (Hebrews 12:15, KJV, emphasis added).

The far-reaching effects of bitterness can even be spread to our children, as well as others, if we persist down its toxic path. Romans 12:17a reminds us, *"Never pay back evil with more evil"* (**NLT**). Giving our husbands the cold shoulder or the silent treatment is, in essence, just a quiet display of resentment for past wrongs incurred. Although quiet in nature, it keenly expresses the underlying anger we feel by our coldness. Sometimes speaking no words says all that we refuse to speak more clearly than we could articulate it openly. Doing so, though, only permits an open door for the nature of the carnal man to subtly make its way to the surface, rearing its ugly head.

One of the easiest ways to detect if we're giving way to our old nature is if we're quarrelsome, regularly carry a poor attitude, and readily give way to strife.

> *Finally, all of you should be of one mind. Sympathize with each other. Love each other as brothers and sisters. Be tenderhearted, and keep a humble attitude. Don't repay evil for evil. Don't retaliate with insults when people insult you. Instead, pay them back with a blessing. That is what God has called you to do, and he will grant you his blessing. For the Scriptures say, "If you want to enjoy life and see many happy days, keep your tongue from speaking evil and your lips from telling lies. Turn away from evil and do good. Search for peace, and work to maintain it. The eyes of the Lord watch over those who do right, and his ears are open to their prayers. But the Lord turns his face against those who do evil.* (1 Peter 3:8–12, NLT)

Until we abandon any prideful pursuit of standing our ground to prove our point, defending ourselves or our own correctness, settling the score, or resentful retaliation, and submit instead to the ways of righteousness, we will make repeated trips around the same mountains. We must be willing to resist strife and pursue peace. James 1:20 reminds us, "*Human anger does not produce the righteousness God desires*" (NLT). Stubborn resistance and haughty dispute only pave the way for one more stroll around the mountain.

HERE WE GO AGAIN

Sometimes a redo is required as we make our way through the wilderness wanderings of our lives when we miss the mark at various points along the way.

I felt impressed one year to read the book *How to Win Friends and Influence People* by Dale Carnegie. I was amazed to find that the message contained within its pages spoke volumes to me regarding my past and then current methods of communicating my point. With calm demeanour, the author conveyed his message with such skill, it made no difference at all that many of the references he used were taken not from recent occurrences but events some seventy or more years past. He effectively brought home the much-needed message that what I previously thought to be constructive, worthwhile communication was actually communication failure at its worst. What an eye opener it was to me. It not only pointed out what I'd been doing wrong but gave helpful illustrations and examples of how to properly engage in effective communication. Moreover, I not only felt led to read the book at that point in time but again a year later, and once more a few years after that! Remember the old saying, "If at first you don't succeed, try, try again"? Oh, how I needed that repeated message! Sometimes going around the mountain will mean not a re-do to instill some unchartered area of needed change but a revisiting of some *previous* instruction to help us gain a clearer understanding and enable us to come up higher. Whatever the Lord may reveal to us, we must focus our attention on our own need for change and leave our husbands and their issues to the Lord.

COMPLAIN AND REMAIN

Complain: "To utter expressions of grief; to lament. I will complain in the bitterness of my spirit. To utter expressions of censure or resentment; to murmur; to find fault. To utter expressions of uneasiness, or pain. To charge; to accuse of an offense; to present an accusation against a person to a proper officer."[16] When we complain about the issues we're experiencing, it's the Lord to whom we make complaint.

Even when we're not speaking directly to the Lord but grumbling about some issue to a friend, the Lord still hears it. We sometimes hold the opinion that it's our right to express our frustrations and feelings and proceed to candidly verbalize our woes concerning our husbands. This, though, in either form is in essence an open expression of a lack of gratitude. Numbers 11:1(a) cautions us, saying, *"Soon the people began to complain about their hardship, and the Lord heard everything they said"* (NLT).

When we begin to openly utter expressions of resentment, murmur, find fault, and make accusations about the offenses of our husbands, it's a clear indication of underlying animosity or bitterness. We need desperately to change our focus. There's a vast difference between going to the Lord in prayer, seeking help for an issue, as opposed to taking a long list of complaints to Him, venting our disapproval. Although the children of Israel found themselves in need and in a situation of distress and discomfort, they still had much

---

[16] *Webster's Dictionary 1828*, s.v. "Complain," accessed December 21, 2023, https://webstersdictionary1828.com/Dictionary/complain.

to be thankful for. Although thirsty, they were still free from the four hundred years of bondage under the task master's whip.

We need to redirect our focus from the problem to the Provider and exchange our heavy heart for a heart of praise. Granted, at times it's a *sacrifice* of praise that we bring, but far better a praise yielded from determined effort than a ready complaint from unchecked emotions. Even during times of turmoil or trouble, we need to find something to be thankful for.

We can be thankful that we *have* a husband if nothing else, and grateful that the Lord is working behind the scenes on our behalf. In Philippians 4:6, Paul tells us, "*Be anxious for nothing, but in everything by prayer and supplication, with thanksgiving, let your requests be made known to God.*" It's our prayers, not our complaints, that move the heart of God.

NO LOOKING BACK

Much of the reason we remain bitter is because of unresolved issues we have yet to see change in and that still actively present a problem. There are things the Lord wants you to forget and release to Him. Holding on to them will only lead to more pain and prolonged suffering. Even if we're yet to see the manifestation of a repentant heart or change in our husbands, we can forgive the past and focus our eyes on the promise of the future, knowing that God is faithful to His promises. Bitterness becomes more deeply rooted when we allow the pain of an offence to remain present and active in our thoughts. Paul admonishes us in 2 Corinthians 10:5 to bring *"every thought into captivity to the obedience of Christ."* In Ephesians 4:26–27, we're reminded not to allow the sun to go down on our anger, giving it time to fester and take root, for doing so only gives a mighty foothold to the devil. Mulling a situation over and over again in our minds only serves to deepen the wound and lengthens the cords of bitterness, giving its roots both ample time, as well as fertile soil, in which to grow.

Forgiveness must be extended first, before we can make any headway. We can't attain tomorrow until we let go of yesterday. In Philippians 4:8, Paul tells us how to deflect nagging thoughts and tormenting negativity:

Finally, brethren, whatever things are true, whatever things are noble, whatever things are just, whatever things are pure, whatever things are lovely, whatever things are of good report, if there is any virtue and if there is anything praiseworthy—meditate on these things.

We must purposely redirect our focus from the hurt to the Healer, releasing both the offence and the offender to the Lord. Closing the door on yesterday can go a long way toward finding healing for today. If we will close the door on the pains of the past, we can be freed from the chains of bitterness and released to embark on the life of freedom and goodness that the Lord has planned for us.

BEWARE OF SNAKE BITES

After the children of Israel had been in the wilderness for some time, they became impatient. Weary of the trials on the way, they began to murmur. In Numbers 21, we find the story of serpents in the wilderness that bit the people who had harshly criticized both the Lord and Moses for their troubles. They had allowed their attitude about the situation to lead them into sinful behaviour involving their mouth and their words.

> *Then the people of Israel set out from Mount Hor, taking the road to the Red Sea to go around the land of Edom. But the people grew impatient with the long journey, and they began to speak against God and Moses. "Why have you brought us out of Egypt to die here in the wilderness?" they complained. "There is nothing to eat here and nothing to drink. And we hate this horrible manna!"*
>
> *So the Lord sent poisonous snakes among the people, and many were bitten and died.* (Numbers 21:4–6, NLT)

Our attitude toward people, things, and situations has the potential to cause us great harm if we allow it free course. The children of Israel focused on the lengthy trek of their journey so much so that they began to candidly speak out about what they were feeling, complaining in their impatience and, in so doing, speaking against both the Lord and their given authority.

> *Then the people came to Moses and cried out, "We have sinned by speaking against the LORD and against you. Pray that the LORD will take away the snakes." So Moses prayed for the people.*
>
> *Then the LORD told him, "Make a replica of a poisonous snake and attach it to a pole. All who are bitten will live if they simply look at it!" So Moses made a snake out of bronze and attached it to a pole. Then anyone who was bitten by a snake could look at the bronze snake and be healed!* (Numbers 21:7–9, NLT)

The replica of the serpent represented sin, and the pole represented the cross of Christ. It's only when we look to the Lord, confessing our sin, that we can overcome its poisonous effects. First John 1:9 tells us, *"If we confess our sins, He is faithful and just to forgive us our sins and to cleanse us from all unrighteousness."* Not only will God forgive us when we confess our sinful behaviour, but He's also willing and able to cleanse us from all unrighteous, unbecoming behaviour, and critical attitudes. We must remember too that deliverance often comes in *phases*. When we try to focus on the progress God has already given us, we won't be as eager to complain about how far we have yet to go.

COME TO THE MOUNTAIN

When the children of Israel finally got to a place of rest while *in* the wilderness, it was at the mountain of God. God brought them to the mountain to meet with Him, hear from Him, and find and place their hope and trust in Him. Before going on to the next phase of their deliverance, the children of Israel would need to get closer to the Lord and would need to seek His face. Second Chronicles 7:14 speaks to us, saying, *"if My people who are called by My name will humble themselves, and pray and seek My face, and turn from their wicked ways, then I will hear from heaven, and will forgive their sin and heal their land."*

God gives us clear instruction to the path that can lead us out of the desert seasons of our lives in this passage of scripture. Step one is humility. Proverbs 15:33 tells us, *"The fear of the Lord is the instruction of wisdom, and before honor is humility."* Before we enjoy the blessing of the promise, we will need to become humble. Humility by definition is freedom from pride and arrogance, whereas the definition for the word "humble" states, "submissive; opposed to proud, haughty, arrogant or assuming. to reduce self-dependence; to make meek and submissive to the divine will."[17]

We will have to let go of our pride and stubbornness and be marked instead by meekness in place of arrogance. We have to let go of our own self will and become submissive to God's divine will in all we do and say.

Secondly, we're told to pray and seek God's face: *"If you need wisdom, ask our generous God, and he will give it to you. He will not rebuke you for asking"* (James 1:5, NLT). In the verses preceding this passage, the apostle addresses

---

[17] *Webster's Dictionary 1828*, s.v. "Humility," accessed December 21, 2023, https://webstersdictionary1828.com/Dictionary/humility.

the trials in one's life and the need for patience and the appropriate mindset as they are endured. He then admonishes us to seek God's wisdom for the appropriate manner to handle any situation of difficulty.

Each of us will have a different path to the road of restoration based upon our own set of issues, attitudes, or critical behaviour, but all roads leading to the Promised Land lead to the Lord and His wisdom. Even when we don't understand the road ahead, we can be confident that God will always be at our side and always lead us on to victory (see 2 Corinthians 2:14). The key is trusting God.

Abraham's wife, Sarah, understood the need for and blessing of trusting God. More than once she'd been placed in difficult situations by her beloved husband that could have caused her great harm. Yet because she trusted God with her situation and responded in a submissive manner, God protected her and blessed her.

I remember a time I went up for prayer during a season of struggle in my own marriage. The pastor who prayed for me told me afterwards not to concentrate on trusting my husband to change but instead to place my trust in God.

God knows you, and He knows your husband. He also knows the problems you're facing, how you got there, and how to successfully bring you through to the other side. It's following our own road map and our own methods that leads us around in circles and on to yet one more stroll around the mountain.

Everyone will experience dry seasons in life, but how long we stay there isn't dependent on our husbands' behaviour but on our own. If we will refrain from unruly debate and unthankful complaints, we can pass through the wilderness season much more quickly. We must be willing to yield to the Lord at the very first notice of improper behaviour, saying, "Not my will, Lord, but *Thy will* be done," allowing Him to redirect our tone, attitude, and behaviour in the proper direction. James 4:6-10 tells us:

> *And he gives grace generously. As the Scriptures say, "God opposes the proud but favors the humble." So humble yourselves before God. Resist the devil, and he will flee from you. Come close to God, and God will come close to you. Wash your hands, you sinners; purify your hearts, for your loyalty is divided between God and the world. Let there be tears for what you have done. Let there be sorrow and deep grief. Let there be sadness instead of laughter, and gloom instead of joy. Humble yourselves before the Lord, and he will lift you up in honor.* (NLT)

It is when we refrain from obstinate willfulness and from pressing on ever forward in our own way of doing and being right that we will make progress in the right direction.

We will need, also, to repent of all negative thoughts and attitudes we've harboured against our husbands and their behaviour. The length of our stay in the desert season is dependent upon how long *we* resist change. Once we come to the mountain and allow God to bring about the necessary changes within us personally, we will begin to see the changes we desire to see in our husbands. What took the children of Israel forty years needed to only take eleven days. It was their attitude and behaviour that kept them in the wilderness for so long.

Take time to survey for possible hardness in your own heart. Don't be the one to hold up progress. We must come to the realization that it may sometimes be our own sinful pride that stalls our progress and submit both our attitude and our will over to the Lord. The sooner we get in step with God and His ways of doing and being right, the sooner we'll be on our way through the wilderness and on to the Promised Land.

So humble yourselves under the mighty power of God, and at the right time he will lift you up in honor. Give all your worries and cares to God, for he cares about you (1 Peter 5:6–7, NLT).

SCRIPTURE CONFESSIONS

"And why worry about a speck in your friend's eye when you have a log in your own? How can you think of saying to your friend, 'Let me help you get rid of that speck in your eye,' when you can't see past the log in your own eye? Hypocrite! First get rid of the log in your own eye; then you will see well enough to deal with the speck in your friend's eye." (Matthew 7:3–5, NLT)

Finally, all of you should be of one mind. Sympathize with each other. Love each other as brothers and sisters. Be tenderhearted, and keep a humble attitude. Don't repay evil for evil. Don't retaliate with insults when people insult you. Instead, pay them back with a blessing. That is what God has called you to do, and he will grant you his blessing. For the Scriptures say, "If you want to enjoy life and see many happy days, keep your tongue from speaking evil and your lips from telling lies. Turn away from evil and do good. Search for peace, and work to maintain it. The eyes of the Lord watch over those who do right, and his ears are open to their prayers. But the Lord turns his face against those who do evil." (1 Peter 3:8–12, NLT)

And "don't sin by letting anger control you." Don't let the sun go down while you are still angry, for anger gives a foothold to the devil. (Ephesians 4:26–27, NLT)

Finally, brethren, whatever things are true, whatever things are noble, whatever things are just, whatever things are pure, whatever things are lovely, whatever things are of good report, if there is any virtue and if there is anything praiseworthy—meditate on these things. (Philippians 4:8)

Dear Heavenly Father,

I ask You to help me to see the flaws within myself before seeing flaws within my husband. Please help me to recognize the areas where I have missed the mark and be quick to yield to

You for correction. Help me to be sympathetic toward my husband, not being critical but readily extending understanding.

Please help me to keep a humble attitude toward him, not repaying evil for evil, but to make effort to bless him in some meaningful way instead. Help me not to give way to anger but to seek peace and pursue to maintain it in our home. Help me to be thankful for, and focus on, what You have already done instead of meditating on what is still in need of correcting.

In Jesus' name, Amen

CHAPTER SEVEN

BELIEVE THE GOOD REPORT

After looking at ourselves, realizing the necessity for our own personal adjustments and modification, combined with the need for change also to be made within our husbands, we may begin to lose hope of ever experiencing a brighter tomorrow, being overwhelmed by the bigness of our need. We can begin to see the issues within each other and in our marriage as giants that are too big to fight, and our hope may begin to wane.

In the previous chapter, we read about the serpents in the wilderness and the weariness of the people as they travelled toward the Land of Promise. In the preceding verses, however, of that very same passage of Scripture, we read about a battle fought and a victory won, just *prior* to their outburst of complaint, which led to their bout with the serpents.

> *The Canaanite king of Arad, who lived in the Negev, heard that the Israelites were approaching on the road through Atharim. So he attacked the Israelites and took some of them as prisoners. Then the people of Israel made this vow to the Lord: "If you will hand these people over to us, we will completely destroy all their towns." The Lord heard the Israelites' request and gave them victory over the Canaanites. The Israelites completely destroyed them and their towns, and the place has been called Hormah ever since. Then the people of Israel set out from Mount Hor, taking the road to the Red Sea to go around the land of Edom. But the people grew impatient with the long journey.* (Numbers 21:1–4, NLT)

It wasn't until after they had begun to fight, even having attained a measure of victory, that they had become weary. Having endured various obstacles, a period of waiting and wondering, as well as unexpected enemies to be fought and overcome, they grew impatient and began to faint. They were prepared to experience *some* degree of difficulty, but they weren't prepared for the magnitude of the struggles they would face. They had expected their journey to be a direct line to the land of milk and honey and were none too happy to find that the road would be paved with roadblocks, setbacks, and battles along the way. They began to wonder if their trials would beat them down and wipe them out before ever setting foot in the Promised Land, and they became disillusioned. Yet, in looking at our Scripture reference from Numbers 21:4, we see that having given them the victory in the battle with the Canaanite King of Arad, the territory they'd conquered was ever thereafter called "Hormah," which means "complete destruction." God will conquer our enemies for us as well as utterly destroy them.

Although we may at times have to stand against them in battle, we can always be assured of victory over our enemies. We cannot become fainthearted at the necessity to face battle, nor allow ourselves to become disillusioned or bewildered by their magnitude. Numbers 13 tells us the story of the men of Israel sent out to spy the Land of Promise. Once there, they witnessed the beauty and provision of the land for themselves, but having seen the size and enormity of its current inhabitants, they became uneasy and began to fear, not remembering their recent victory or the promise of the similar destruction of *all* their enemies, both present, as well as future.

> *After exploring the land for forty days, the men returned to Moses, Aaron, and the whole community of Israel at Kadesh in the wilderness of Paran. They reported to the whole community what they had seen and showed them the fruit they had taken from the land. This was their report to Moses: "We entered the land you sent us to explore, and it is indeed a bountiful country—a land flowing with milk and honey. Here is the kind of fruit it produces. But the people living there are powerful, and their towns are large and fortified. We even saw giants there, the descen-*

dants of Anak! The Amalekites live in the Negev, and the Hittites, Jebusites, and Amorites live in the hill country. The Canaanites live along the coast of the Mediterranean Sea and along the Jordan Valley."

But Caleb tried to quiet the people as they stood before Moses. "Let's go at once to take the land," he said. "We can certainly conquer it!"

But the other men who had explored the land with him disagreed. "We can't go up against them! They are stronger than we are!" So they spread this bad report about the land among the Israelites: "The land we traveled through and explored will devour anyone who goes to live there. All the people we saw were huge. We even saw giants there, the descendants of Anak. Next to them we felt like grasshoppers, and that's what they thought, too!" (Numbers 13:25–33, NLT)

They had focused more on the problem than on the promise, and upon the battle more than believing.

IS THERE ANYTHING TOO HARD FOR GOD?

Early in our marriage, we felt like the Lord had told us we would have a marriage that others would want. That was both exciting as well as comforting. We knew from the start that our marriage was to be a beautiful one. So when we started to see things surface that weren't expected, we were confused.

On the heels of that unexpected trip to the hospital that dashed our dreams of adding to our family, I began experiencing some health issues. What I thought was possibly strep throat was diagnosed as thyroid cancer. I had never thought to hear those words in conjunction with me. I was in shock. Dale had been with me for the diagnosis. What I assumed was a routine trip to the doctor for a prescription for my sore throat turned out to be only the start of a very long trip down a road I had never seen coming. Sickness can separate us in ways you never dreamed. I had three closely coupled hospital stays, and an order to *stay away* from my husband and family for a lengthy period of time due to radiation treatment—wanting to be close yet being kept at a distance under mandatory restriction. I had come through the surgery, but the period of recovery wouldn't be easy. I began to wonder if we would ever even make it to our ever after, or would we be stopped in our tracks?

A major health issue can be very hard on a marriage in many ways, emotionally as well as financially, just like an ugly custody battle or the new-found knowledge of a cheating spouse can be. The three Cs—cheating, child custody, and cancer—are the big ones that can threaten the very fabric of any marriage if allowed.

We don't see these things coming, and all at once we're in a battle that we're not sure we can win, and one we're not sure how to fight. We see a giant before us and become bewildered. We're expecting smooth sailing but instead are met with obstacles of monstrous size, and so become angry and begin to think, *This is not what I signed up for.*

Sometimes when we look at the magnitude of the problems we face, they seem too big to overcome. When we're starry-eyed and in love, on our way *to* matrimony, we can only envision the promise of a life of love and happiness—the milk and honey, not the muck and the mire—and we want to run. But we *did* sign up for whatever journey is set before us when we promised, at the very same altar, for better *or* for worse. We are to be all in, even when challenged with enemies we would rather not face.

This is when we have to remember the promises of God for our lives. Even if you don't have a specific word from the Lord, we can claim and hold on to the promises given to His children in His Word. We are told that there is nothing impossible for the Lord to handle, even if it looms large in our minds and thoughts. God can fell a giant with one tiny stone. If we will give Him the faith of a mustard seed, we can see giant obstacles fall at our feet, if we only believe.

On the car ride home from the doctor's office following the diagnosis, I just sat there. The ride was silent all the way home. Neither of us said a word. It occurred to me that I should be crying, but no tears came until we were almost home. The peace of the Lord was upon me. He was letting me know that everything would be ok. I didn't know what the road ahead would look like, but I knew that the Lord was right there with me, all the way.

That diagnosis came in 2006, and I'm cancer free! Thank You, Jesus! God fought that giant battle for me, defeated my enemy completely, and set me back on my feet to continue along the road to our happily ever after.

WHOSE REPORT WILL YOU BELIEVE?

The enemy is all too happy to give you a report of doom and imminent defeat, but is it his report, or the report of the Lord that you will believe? Part of the problem lies in the fact that instead of immediately choosing to align with the Word of the Lord, the children of Israel chose instead to dwell on the thought of battle rather than receive the positive report and take action. In Numbers 13:30, we read, *"But Caleb tried to quiet the people as they stood before Moses. 'Let's go at once to take the land,' he said. 'We can certainly conquer it!'"* (NLT).

The passage goes on to say that the other men *disagreed* with him. They refused to come into agreement with the promise and listened instead to the voice of doubt, choosing to fixate only on the negative, allowing it to steal away their hope. Sometimes when we see yet another crisis to face, we set up camp in a place of inactivity. We dread the thought of yet one more conflict. This, although a temporary escape from confrontation, leads only to defeat.

Dread: "to be very unwilling to face; great fear especially of something that will or *might* happen."[18]

Deuteronomy 1:29b tells us, *"Dread not, neither be afraid of them"* (KJV). Instead of receiving the good

---

[18] *Webster's Canadian Dictionary & Thesaurus*, s.v. "Dread," accessed December 21, 2023, https://archive.org/details/websterscanadian0000unse/page/n5/mode/2up.

report and acting on it, they chose instead to fear the giants, causing them to spend the next forty years in the wilderness. God had shown them the fruit of the land and the overwhelming blessing and provision it held, yet they chose to focus not on the goodness of the land, but upon the obstacles that surrounded it. We, too, do similarly when we allow the issues we face to cloud our view of the promises that have been spoken regarding our men and our marriages.

UNSEEN HOPE

Admittedly, it can be difficult at times to continue to trudge through when all you see before you screams the very opposite of what you're believing for. In Romans 8:24, Paul reminds us of what it means to truly hope: *"For we were saved in this hope, but hope that is seen is not hope; for why does one still hope for what he sees?"* God tells us here in His Word that we will not always clearly see the desired outcome at the onset, and we most likely will not, but not to place our hope in what we see but in the promise that may not be clearly seen, for it will not fail. Romans 8:25 declares, *"But if we hope for what we do not see, we eagerly wait for it with perseverance."*

Perseverance: "Steady persistence in a course of action, a purpose, a state, etc. especially in spite of difficulties, obstacles or discouragement."[19] We must stay the course and persevere! Our marriages are worth fighting for.

---

[19] *Webster's Universal College Dictionary*, s.v. "Perseverance," accessed December 21, 2023, https://archive.org/details/webstersuniversa0000unse_p5e0/page/n5/mode/2up.

GO AGAIN

Then Elijah said to Ahab, "Go get something to eat and drink, for I hear a mighty rainstorm coming!"

So Ahab went to eat and drink. But Elijah climbed to the top of Mount Carmel and bowed low to the ground and prayed with his face between his knees.

Then he said to his servant, "Go and look out toward the sea."

The servant went and looked, then returned to Elijah and said, "I didn't see anything."

Seven times Elijah told him to go and look. Finally the seventh time, his servant told him, "I saw a little cloud about the size of a man's hand rising from the sea."

Then Elijah shouted, "Hurry to Ahab and tell him, 'Climb into your chariot and go back home. If you don't hurry, the rain will stop you!'"

And soon the sky was black with clouds. A heavy wind brought a terrific rainstorm, and Ahab left quickly for Jezreel. (1 Kings 18:41–45, NLT)

This passage tells us the story of perseverance and the power of confident believing. No matter how small the progress, no matter how many times you must look to see any sign of change, believe that change is on the horizon. Remember the cloud the size of a man's hand and the abundance of blessing that followed it. There may not have been much to go on, naturally speaking, but the fullness of the blessing wasn't contained in the small cloud but in what came after it—a huge downpour of blessing!

Begin to thank God for the small things, and the abundance will follow. Gratitude and a thankful heart can be seeds sown for the overflow. Even if the major issues still arise, thank God for the progress that has been made, no matter how small, and soon you will hear the sound of the abundance of rain.

In Romans 4:18–21, Paul tells us:

Even when there was no reason for hope, Abraham kept hoping—believing that he would become the father of many nations. For God had said to him, "That's how many descendants you will have!" And Abraham's faith did not weaken, even though, at about 100 years of age, he figured his body was as good as dead—and so was Sarah's womb.

Abraham never wavered in believing God's promise. In fact, his faith grew stronger, and in this he brought glory to God. He was fully convinced that God is able to do whatever he promises. (NLT)

The pastor who married my husband and I used to say to the saints on a regular basis, as a constant encouragement to us, "God said it, I believe it, and that settles it!"

DON'T GET WEARY

Scripture tells us in Galatians 6:9, "*So let's not get tired of doing what is good. At just the right time we will reap a harvest of blessing if we don't give up*" (NLT). We must believe that beyond the battle there is victory, and that God *will* give us the victory over the battle. We must believe that we will both enter into *and enjoy* the place of rest that's been promised. Don't allow the battles of life to steal your hope.

Hebrews 10:35–36 tells us:

So do not throw away this confident trust in the Lord. Remember the great reward it brings you! Patient endurance is what you need now, so that you will continue to do God's will. Then you will receive all that he has promised. (NLT)

Don't throw away your confidence. Don't waste time looking at the size of the giants in your life. Don't look at the bigness of your problem; look at the bigness of your God! With just one smooth stone, young David toppled the giant that stood before him. But it wasn't the stone that brought the giant down—it was David's faith in God. Because David believed God would deliver Goliath into his hands, God gave him the victory! Believe the good report!

Believe: "To credit upon the authority or testimony of another; to be persuaded of the truth of something upon the declaration of another, to expect or hope with confidence; to trust."[20]

---

[20] *Webster's Dictionary 1828*, s.v. "Believe," accessed December 21, 2023, https://webstersdictionary1828.com/Dictionary/believe.

SCRIPTURE CONFESSIONS

Even when there was no reason for hope, Abraham kept hoping—believing that he would become the father of many nations. For God had said to him, "That's how many descendants you will have!" And Abraham's faith did not weaken, even though, at about 100 years of age, he figured his body was as good as dead—and so was Sarah's womb. Abraham never wavered in believing God's promise. In fact, his faith grew stronger, and in this he brought glory to God. He was fully convinced that God is able to do whatever he promises. (Romans 4:18–21, NLT)

So let's not get tired of doing what is good. At just the right time we will reap a harvest of blessing if we don't give up. (Galatians 6:9, NLT)

So do not throw away this confident trust in the Lord. Remember the great reward it brings you! Patient endurance is what you need now, so that you will continue to do God's will. Then you will receive all that he has promised. (Hebrews 10:35–36, NLT)

Father God in Heaven,

Please help me to have hope even when things don't look hopeful in the natural. Help me not to waver in believing for Your promise of intervention but be unwavering, being fully convinced that what You promise, You will do.

Please keep me from growing weary in the wait, and help me to endure, with full assurance of Your salvation. Help me to continue to do Your will in all things. I choose to believe the good report; I choose to stand upon Your Word. I thank You that, at just the right time, You will cause me to reap the harvest of blessing as You have promised, for You are faithful.

In Jesus' name, Amen.

CHAPTER EIGHT

Taking Jericho

Then Joshua rose early in the morning; and they set out from Acacia Grove and came to the Jordan, he and all the children of Israel, and lodged there before they crossed over. So it was, after three days, that the officers went through the camp; and they commanded the people, saying, "When you see the ark of the covenant of the LORD your God, and the priests, the Levites, bearing it, then you shall set out from your place and go after it. Yet there shall be a space between you and it, about two thousand cubits by measure. Do not come near it, that you may know the way by which you must go, for you have not passed this way before." (Joshua 3:1–4)

PREPARING FOR BATTLE

Preparation: "The act or operation of preparing or fitting for a particular purpose, use, service, or condition; as the preparation of land for a crop of wheat; the preparation of troops for a campaign; the preparation of a nation for war; the preparation of men for future happiness. Preparation is intended to prevent evil or secure good."[21]

---

[21] *Webster's Dictionary 1828*, s.v. "Preparation," accessed December 21, 2023, https://webstersdictionary1828.com/Dictionary/preparation.

The word "preparation" as defined above has two objectives: to prevent evil and/or secure good. Just as getting a proper night's rest can be beneficial in preparing for that big test or important business meeting the following morning, proper preparation by way of adequate rest can also help to ward off inappropriate behaviour, thus *preventing evil*.

When we are tired and worn out, we're more prone to mistakes and irritability. Have you ever heard the expression "hangry?" It's the place between being hungry and becoming angry, and can, and often does, promote irritable behavior. Similarly, when we're stressed out, or pressed to the point of frustration, we're more inclined to lash out and less likely to wait for instruction, or even seek it. When we're frequently in a state of turmoil or experiencing underlying emotional strain, we're much less likely to handle a given situation in the appropriate manner. Taking proper rest can give us time to clear our heads and prepare our hearts to engage the situation with the proper mindset, attitude, and approach. Both can go a long way toward securing the good of our future happiness.

KNOW THYSELF

Irritable: "very susceptible of anger or passion; easily inflamed or exasperated; as an irritable temper."[22]

When I'm tired or hungry, I'm more prone to irritability, or leaning on the fleshly nature. I've come to know myself in this regard. Knowing your pressure points can

---

[22] *Webster's Dictionary 1828*, s.v. "Irritable," accessed December 21, 2023, https://webstersdictionary1828.com/Dictionary/irritable.

go a long way toward heading off fits of temper or emotional outburst, before they make their way out into the open, thus shutting down possible conflict before it starts.

By taking inventory of our own personal pressure points ahead of time, we can begin to recognize them when they press at us beneath the surface. We can then purpose to remain peaceful and pleasant, instead of allowing the pressure to cause us to explode, unloading words and emotions that only serve to bring conflict. I'm sad to say that I have gotten myself into more than a few messes on some occasions.

What I'd like to point out is this—when we know that we become irritable if we're hungry, stressed, or tired, and we feel these emotions begin to rise to the surface, we can simply stop, recognize what's happening, and choose *on purpose* to go in another direction. Simply choose not to engage in important issues and conversations until you've had time to rest, refuel, and be refreshed. If you already know that you become irritable when you're tired, and you've been working for twelve hours nonstop, shut it down for the day. If you know you get angry when you haven't eaten, and the meeting went an hour past lunch, get something to eat before going on to do more. If you've had a pressure-filled week and feel stressed and overworked, make it a point to spend some quiet time with the Lord in prayer and devotions so that your spirit can be uplifted before re-engaging in activities.

The enemy knows what buttons to push and is more than happy to create mountains out of molehills if we let him. He's all too ready to create opportunity for an argument that didn't have to start, a word that didn't have to be spoken, or that *split* that just didn't have to happen, and all because we don't allow for times of needed rest and refreshment.

REST FOR THE WEARY

Rest: "rest from labor; rest from mental exertion; rest of body or mind. The mind is at rest when it ceases to be disturbed or agitated." Quiet: "a state free from motion or disturbance; that on which anything leans or lies for support."[23]

In Matthew 11:28, Jesus speaks to us concerning times of trial or distress, saying, *"Come to me, all of you who are weary and carry heavy burdens, and I will give you rest"* (NLT). Not only does Jesus desire that we have physical rest for our bodies, but also for our mind, so that we experience rest from emotional heaviness. The mind is at rest when it ceases to be disturbed or agitated. We can experience the peace that passes all understanding when we *lean on, rely on*, and trust in the Lord to carry the weight of the load we bear.

It is when we cast the burden of our heart at His feet to manage that we will experience a mind free from disturbance and mental agitation. Additionally, we see in our Scripture text that not only did the children of Israel need rest before continuing onward in their pursuit of victory, but it was necessary that their leader,

---

[23] *Webster's Dictionary 1828*, s.v. "Rest," accessed December 21, 2023, https://webstersdictionary1828.com/Dictionary/rest.

Joshua, also take rest at the same time with them: *"Then Joshua rose early in the morning; and they set out from Acacia Grove and came to the Jordan, he and all the children of Israel, and lodged there before they crossed over"* (Joshua 3:1). Sometimes we're so fixated on and preoccupied with our own pain that we forget that our husbands have feelings too. Giving them relief from the weight of *our* heartache can be a significant factor in lifting the burden off their shoulders, freeing them also to move forward in the process of healing. Part of this release can come in the form of releasing them from the guilt and blame of past hurts and offences. Letting them know that we have forgiven them and are willing to let go of the past will be like a breath of fresh air.

Proverbs 27:15-16 reminds us, *"A quarrelsome wife is as annoying as constant dripping on a rainy day. Stopping her complaints is like trying to stop the wind or trying to hold something with greased hands"* (NLT). Constant reminders only stand to alienate our husbands, causing them to put up walls of resentment toward us. Our husbands are much more likely to be open to the idea of moving forward when they know that the past won't be revisited, rehearsed, or revived around the next bend, as may have been the status quo in times past.

There are two main parts to the word "rehearse"—the prefix *re* and the word *hear*. To rehearse means to recount events and to cause a person to re-*hear* something over and over again. Proverbs 14:1 tells us, *"A wise woman builds her home, but a foolish woman tears it down with her own hands*" (NLT). In order to give our husbands rest, we can make the decision to stop rehearsing his flaws and/or repeatedly throwing them in his face, so to speak, and throw them away instead. Tear up the tally sheet and let bygones be bygones. Everyone needs to experience rest from adversity, pain, and sorrow, and everyone needs to be released and freed to advance forward without the threat of perpetual reminders from the past. Solomon in all his wisdom wrote that there is "*A time to tear down and a time to build up*" (Ecclesiastes 3:3b, NLT). The time for criticizing and laying blame for past mistakes is over; the time for restoration and edification has come. Keep necessary conversation and communication limited to *current* issues only.

Edify: "1. To build, in a literal sense. 2. To instruct and improve the mind in knowledge generally and particularly in moral and religious knowledge, in faith and holiness."[24]

We need to build up our husbands and edify them with soothing words of love, forgiveness, and acceptance. When we look to the Word of God for instruction, we can obtain the wisdom we need, but it's only when we apply it that we can have true success.

Let's be wise women and build our homes instead of tearing them down. Refuse to place one more verbal brick of reminder on the wall of opposition and offence.

---

[24] *Webster's Dictionary 1828*, s.v. "Edify," accessed December 21, 2023, https://webstersdictionary1828.com/Dictionary/edify.

A WALLED CITY

Jericho was a strong and fortified city with high walls wide enough to build houses upon. The aim in erecting such walls was to shield its inhabitants from the threat of outside enemy infiltration, while also securing their safety and protection. We too can build walls in our lives in an attempt to keep out the pain of past hurts and sorrow, but those self-same walls can also separate us from that which we desire to allow *in*. Joshua 6:1 states, *"Now the gates of Jericho were tightly shut because the people were afraid of the Israelites. No one was allowed to go out or in"* (NLT).

Any walls we establish for our own security are made in *self*-preservation and *self*-protection—the common denominator being "self." When employed improperly, walls are not only a barrier to what we desire to keep out, but they can also become an unwelcome stumbling block, hindering what we desire to receive in. Proverbs 17:19b reminds us that *"anyone who trusts in high walls invites disaster"* (NLT). Desiring to receive love, we can instead push it away with both hands, hiding behind walls of self-protection against further hurt.

Our security comes from the Lord. Our protection comes from the Lord. He is able to heal any wound we may encounter along our path to victory. We can't allow fear to keep us holed up behind walls of self-protection. Anytime we attempt to protect ourselves, we only bar the way for the intervention of the Lord.

FOLLOW THE LEADER

In taking over that very first territory from their enemy, the children of Israel were given very specific instructions on *how* they should proceed. There was great detail given to Joshua from the Lord, which made up the battle plan for overtaking the city of Jericho. It was not like a typical military command but was quite to the contrary. Although they would have a part to play in the battle, it was the Lord Who would go before them and pave the way for their victory. The fight would not begin with a thunderous charge under cover of night to seize their enemy but in the light of day, *peacefully*. Isaiah 55:9 reminds us, *"For just as the heavens are higher than the earth, so my ways are higher than your ways and my thoughts higher than your thoughts"* (NLT).

Before advancing forward to obtain victory in any given situation, our plan for attacking the issues in our lives will have to give way to those of the Lord. God explained to Joshua the reason behind our need for cautious discretion in our endeavour to advance, saying, *"for you have not passed this way before"* (Joshua 3:4b). He also gave instruction just prior to that statement, saying, *"Stay about a half mile behind them, keeping a clear distance between you and the Ark. Make sure you don't come any closer"* (Joshua 3:4, NLT).

Whenever we are too close to a situation, we don't always have the proper focus of the matter. Our focus may be blurred by any number of factors. Our emotions, for example, can have a vast impact on how we perceive a matter, among other things. We need to pause and allow some space for inquiry and instruction. If we get ahead of the Lord in any pursuit, we run the risk of not furthering our cause but, instead, delaying it or bringing it to a standstill altogether. We don't know which approach to take, so we must purpose to temporarily stop and take time to clearly see and understand the direction in which the Lord would have us proceed. Permitting the proper space to allow for divine guidance will be crucial. This pause for direction bears resemblance to the action we're asked to take in our next step in advancement—submission. Submission is the act of yielding *our* own will for the will of another.

Submission/submissive/submissiveness: "The act of yielding to power or authority; surrender of the person and power to the control or government of another. Obedience; compliance with the commands or laws of a superior. Submission of children to their parents is an indispensable duty. A yielding of one's will to the will or appointment of a superior without murmuring. A submissive temper or disposition."[25]

For us as wives, submission is twofold in the process of the restoration of our marriages. We will first have to submit and yield to the leadership of the Lord, following His lead, and then, as He has required of us, yield also to the leadership of our husbands: *"Wives, likewise, be submissive to your own husbands"* (1 Peter 3:1a). We often say, "I'll follow the *Lord*, but following my husband is quite a different story."

---

[25] *Webster's Dictionary 1828*, s.v. "Submission," accessed December 21, 2023, https://webstersdictionary1828.com/Dictionary/submission.

While submission *is* the act of yielding, it is never control. It does not mean that you have no voice or opinion in matters of your home, and it is never to be used as a means of manipulation. We always have a voice and are by no means to be dismissed, devalued, or disregarded. We are equals in the marriage union and as such should always have a role in the decision-making process.

Wifely submission in its simplest form is, as the later portion of the definition states, *a submissive temper or disposition*. First Peter 3:4 emphasizes this aspect in this way: *"You should clothe yourselves instead with the beauty that comes from within, the unfading beauty of a gentle and quiet spirit, which is so precious to God"* (NLT). Submission at its core is the absence of an argumentative or domineering attitude. The willingness to yield to leadership, forgoing rebellious confrontation, is precious to the Lord.

ORDER, ORDER!

Without a structure of authority there would only be chaos and confusion. Paul reminds us in 1 Corinthians 14:33a: *"For God is not a God of disorder but of peace"* (NLT). There must be order in any given structure, be it government, the workplace, the educational system, and, yes, even in the home. Both husband and wife are equal in the marriage union, but for the purpose of maintaining order in the home, God has established the husband as the head of the family.

And further, submit to one another out of reverence for Christ.

For wives, this means submit to your husbands as to the Lord. For a husband is the head of his wife as Christ is the head of the church. He is the Savior of his body, the church. As the church submits to Christ, so you wives should submit to your husbands in everything. (Ephesians 5:21–24, NLT)

This is how the holy women of old made themselves beautiful. They put their trust in God and accepted the authority of their husbands. For instance, Sarah obeyed her husband, Abraham, and called him her master. You are her daughters when you do what is right without fear of what your husbands might do. (1 Peter 3:5–6, NLT)

God has asked us to submit to our husbands' authority as in obedience to *His* authority. Yes, our husbands may make mistakes along the way, where the Lord never will, but we as wives are not judged by the outcome of the act of submission, only by our obedience *to* it. Order in the home is yet another way that strife and argumentation is derailed. If we lovingly submit to one another's needs, opinions, and desires, the possibility of conflict is greatly minimized, and peace instead of chaos can be the established norm.

THE FORMULA FOR SUCCESS

The next aspect in the battle plan for success is also found in one word—"grace." The only way we can successfully submit to any authority is through the power of God's grace.

Grace: "Favorable influence of God; divine influence or the influence of the spirit, in renewing the heart and restraining from sin,"[26] or, as defined in the *Strong's Concordance of the Bible*, "the divine influence upon the heart and its reflection in the life."[27]

Jesus gave us great insight into our need for absolute dependence upon Him when He told us, "*I am the vine, you are the branches. He who abides in Me, and I in him, bears much fruit; for without Me you can do nothing*" (John 15:5). In Colossians 1:27b, Paul tells us that it's "*Christ in you, the hope of glory*" (KJV). It is Christ in us, the hope of acting right, speaking right, or doing right.

It is only when we wholly lean and rely on the Lord and His free gift of grace (His divine influence upon and operational in our lives) that we are able to attain any measure of success whatsoever. Through the gift of grace, our own effort is replaced with God's power! The only way to sure victory is to let go and let God!

In Romans 11:6, Paul gives us a further description saying, "*But if it is of grace, then it is no longer of works: or grace would not be grace*" (BBE). In the same way that oil and water don't mix, grace and our own self effort can't be combined to produce the desired outcome of any situation. Our entire dependence must be upon God and

---

[26] *Webster's Dictionary 1828*, s.v. "Grace," accessed December 21, 2023, https://webstersdictionary1828.com/Dictionary/grace.

[27] James Strong, *The New Strong's Exhaustive Concordance of the Bible*, s.v. "grace" (Nashville, TN: Thomas Nelson Publishers, 1990).

God alone. Just as the children of Israel had to follow behind the Ark, we will have to follow along God's path and at His pace for our own progress. The first steps in the right direction, once we've yielded our hearts and attitudes, are those taken in grace.

Grace is also an aspect of the rest of God. "Rest," as we've read, can refer to something on which something, or someone, leans or lies on for support. Grace is wholly leaning on the power and ability of the Lord to move on our behalf and lead in the details of our everyday life in every way. Grace is our formula for success! Hebrews 4:16 gives us the answer key saying, *"Let us therefore come boldly to the throne of grace, that we may obtain mercy and find grace to help in time of need."* Instead of finding boldness in ourselves to exert our own will and authority, we must go boldly to God, seeking and asking for His divine influence to be manifested in every area of our lives.

SILENT VICTORY

When it was time for the children of Israel to, in fact, begin their advance forward, God didn't tell them to simply charge into Jericho full steam ahead with force, but instead gave them deliberate instruction to approach the city peacefully and in silence. For seven days they were told to march around the city without making a sound. Again, the number seven appears here too, representing the aspect of completion, and once again in the form of surrender and compliance. Would the children of Israel again rebel at the command given by the Lord, protesting the method instructed of approaching the city? Or would they submit in silence, allowing the Lord to go ahead of them and give them the victory in His own way? The opposite of submission is resistance. We can display resistance with an unwillingness to yield to direction, refusal to hold our peace, or blatant defiance to given instruction.

Resistance: "The act of resisting; opposition. Resistance is passive, as that of a fixed body which interrupts the passage of a moving body; or active, as in the exertion of force to stop, repel or defeat progress or designs; that power of a body which acts in opposition to the impulse or pressure of another, or which prevents the effect of another power."[28] As we have seen so often, yielding to our own will only hinders our progress.

By obediently walking around the city for seven days without making a sound, the children of Israel had shown that they no longer desired to take action in their own way. They were now ready to submit to the leadership and authority of their God and follow His lead. We are made ready to advance when we are ready to follow in obedience.

A portion of the definition for the word "preparation" states, "as the preparation of land for a crop of wheat; or the preparation of troops for a campaign." Scripture gives us further detail in the significance of this: *"I tell you the truth, unless a kernel of wheat is planted in the soil and dies, it remains alone. But its death will produce many*

---

[28] *Webster's Dictionary 1828*, s.v. "Resistance," accessed December 21, 2023, https://webstersdictionary1828.com/Dictionary/resistance.

new kernels—a plentiful harvest of new lives" (John 12:24, NLT). When we die to our flesh, submit to the Lord, and rest in the knowledge and understanding that God is on our side, willing and able to defend and protect us, we will see the kind of fruit produced in our lives and in our marriages that we have been seeking.

As they walked calmly and quietly around the enormous walls of opposition that stood before them, their enemy became all the more aware of the awesome power of their God. By entering silently in submission, they displayed that it was not in their own power and authority that they would enter the city, but in the Lord's.

In Philippians 1:28, Paul reminds us, *"Don't be intimidated in any way by your enemies. This will be a sign to them that they are going to be destroyed, but that you are going to be saved, even by God himself"* (NLT). Again, it's not our *husbands* that the Lord is out to undo but the hand of the enemy at work within our marriages. In Exodus 14:14 we find, *"The Lord will fight for you, and you shall hold your peace."*

SING HALLELUJAH!

After walking around the walls of Jericho, the children of Israel were then instructed to make a shout of victory. They were told to shout *before* the walls fell down before them. It wasn't until after the waters were parted at the Red Sea that the children of Israel sang their song of deliverance to the Lord, but they had already been assured of the victory beforehand. They could have begun to sing as they stood at the water's edge, but it wasn't until they watched the horse and rider fall into the sea that they began to sing. How beautiful if we could get to the place where we begin to sing God's praise before we see the victory, showing our trust in Him in the here and now.

As soon as they made the shout of victory, the once enormous walls of opposition fell at their feet, paving the way to sure victory. We can begin to praise the Lord before we see anything in the natural that would indicate a shift in our situation. Psalm 103:1 tells us, *"Bless the L*ORD*, O my soul; and all that is within me, bless His holy name!"* Our soul is made up of our mind, our will, and our emotions. When we make the conscious decision to override our emotions and instead decide to bless the Lord, we are choosing to praise Him regardless of our current circumstances, what our emotions may be screaming at us, or what our mind may have to say about the situation.

We already know the victory is sure. Lift your eyes up to the Lord in the face of any walls of hurt or rejection you may be feeling, knowing that, just like the walls of Jericho, whatever wall stands before you must bow and crumble at the Word of the Lord!

In closing out this chapter, it seems good to encourage you with the words of the apostle Peter: *"Grace and peace be multiplied to you in the knowledge of God and of Jesus our Lord"* (2 Peter 1:2). Multiplied grace is what we are in need of. The multiplied peace of God is what is required. These are the pass keys to victory—peace to wait upon the Lord, and His grace abounding in our soul (our mind, will, and emotions) as we await the promised victory.

As Jericho was only the first city to be taken by the Israelites, it gives us the much-needed reminder that change and advancement will take time. The children of Israel were promised a great deal of territory, and they would take it one town and one city at a time. We too will need to proceed one step at a time. If we will begin to yield to God and honour the Lord, becoming submissive to His Will and direction, we will find that our advancement will progress at a much faster pace. Just as the children of Israel had to follow behind the Ark, we will have to follow along at God's pace and in His wisdom for our progress and advancement. We will need to stay close enough to the Lord to hear His direction, far enough away from the situation to allow Him to lead us, and submissive enough to do as He commands. Grace and peace be multiplied unto you!

SCRIPTURE CONFESSIONS

A wise woman builds her home, but a foolish woman tears it down with her own hands. (Proverbs 14:1, NLT)

This is how the holy women of old made themselves beautiful. They put their trust in God and accepted the authority of their husbands. For instance, Sarah obeyed her husband, Abraham, and called him her master. You are her daughters when you do what is right without fear of what your husbands might do. (1 Peter 3:5–6, NLT)

"The Lord will fight for you, and you shall hold your peace." (Exodus 14:14)

Dear Father God in Heaven,

Please help me to be a wise woman, not foolishly tearing down my home and my marriage by my own doing, but being as the holy women of old, trusting You completely. Help me to hold my tongue from fruitless argumentation and from fighting my battles in my own way, allowing You to fight them for me instead. Help me to accept the authority of my husband and be respectful of him, not being afraid of what he might do, knowing that I can trust You in all things, and that You are faithful.

In Jesus' name, Amen.

CHAPTER NINE

DECLARING THE VICTORY

"Be strong and of good courage, for to this people you shall divide as an inheritance the land which I swore to their fathers to give them. Only be strong and very courageous, that you may observe to do according to all the law which Moses My servant commanded you; do not turn from it to the right hand or to the left, that you may prosper wherever you go. This Book of the Law shall not depart from your mouth, but you shall meditate in it day and night, that you may observe to do according to all that is written in it. For then you will make your way prosperous, and then you will have good success." (Joshua 1:6–8)

THREE STEPS TO VICTORY

The answers we need are given to us at the beginning of God's command to Joshua to take the children of Israel across the Jordan and into the Promised Land. Joshua was given three steps to obtain the victory before ever sending him forward: (1) *"This Book of the Law shall not depart from your mouth;"* (2) *"meditate in it day and night;"* (3) *"observe to do according to all that is written in it.*" God always has a blueprint for our success, even before we begin on our journey.

SPEAK THE WORD

At the top of the list is the reminder to keep the Word of God on his lips. In other words, he was told to continually speak in alignment with God's Word. Joshua was not to speak what he saw in the natural, nor to speak what he felt in his emotions, or be intimidated with fear; instead, he was to speak what God had already said in all situations. If he focused on what he had seen before him, he would only observe a huge barrier of opposition standing in the way of his advancement. Instead of saying, "God, there's a huge wall in front of us. There's no way we can get through this," he was told to say what God had already told him about the situation. The land belonged to them and was theirs for the taking.

Joshua had not come into agreement with the other ten spies who had gone out to spy the land the first time around, who had only seen the problem. In fact, he had already been believing and speaking that it was indeed possible to take the land for some time. He had been planting and watering the seed of faith before ever reaching the walls of Jericho. We too will need to spend some time sowing seeds of faith. We may even sow through tears in times of our greatest struggles. We must remember that seeds take time to germinate.

In a previous chapter, I began to tell you about one of the giant obstacles my husband and I faced when what I thought to be a simple ailment turned out instead to be cancer. The car ride home was silent, yes, but when we got home, I began to talk to my husband about the unseen road ahead of us. I asked him to do something for me from the very beginning. I asked him not to tell anyone what I was dealing with. "Don't tell anyone that it's cancer." No one meant absolutely no one. I asked him only to give details of my progress. She had to have surgery today. She came through surgery well. She needs another surgery. She has to go back in once more. No *why* behind the what. Let me explain.

SOMETHING TO TALK ABOUT

Have you ever heard the saying, "If you can't say anything nice, don't say anything at all"? Even though I didn't know what the road ahead of me would look like, I knew the mindset that typically followed that particular "c" word. I was believing God from the very start for my healing, and I didn't want words of negativity circulating about me or my condition. I only wanted to plant seeds of faith. No matter what lay ahead, I only wanted to speak what I wanted the outcome to be. I only wanted to believe.

I recently watched a movie for the very first time titled *Breakthrough*. It's the story of a young boy who fell through the ice and was trapped beneath it for several minutes. The prognosis wasn't good. When his mother came into the room where her child lay lifeless, she refused to believe what she saw before her. Instead of speaking what she saw, she prayed and asked the Lord to bring life back into her child's body. Immediately there was a change. He now had a pulse and was breathing again, when minutes before the doctor and team had given up hope. Same prognosis, mind you, but now there was a sign of hope. They would have an intense three days ahead of them, but the Lord healed her son completely. No loss of brain function, no paralysis whatsoever. Nothing that had been previously diagnosed as his possible outcome! Amen!

When people hear of bad news, they often speak words that are meant to comfort, or be of kind advice, but are instead words that instill doubt, fear, and unbelief. Things like, "Oh girl, if your husband cheated, you need to cut him loose for your own sake." How about, "You can't expect to have a happy marriage caring for another woman's child under your roof." Or like in the movie, "If the situation is that far gone, then we just need to be here for support until the inevitable happens."

When the boy's mother overheard the doctors talking about the negative prognosis by her son's bedside, and their family and friends speaking words of doom just down the hall, she basically asked them plain and simple, "If you aren't going to speak life over my son, then please just leave!" We serve a miracle-working God no matter what the prognosis. If your marriage looks dead, then call it back to life in the name of Jesus! Speak to the dry bones of a disconnect and separation and tell them to come back together again in the name of Jesus!

Speak the Word of God over your situation, no matter how dead it looks!

In the movie, it would be days before seeing any real signs of life in her son, but she planted God's Word by faith into the situation. Plant the seed of the Word of God instead of doubt and unbelief over your marriage, water it with praise and with prayer, and watch God bring you a harvest of a restored marriage better than new! We must keep in mind the law of seed, time, and harvest.

First, we need to plant the right seed, give God some time with the situation, and then we reap the harvest. Psalm 126:5–6 encourages us: *"Those who plant in tears will harvest with shouts of joy. They weep as they go to plant their seed, but they sing as they return with the harvest"* (NLT). Don't allow the Word of God to depart from your mouth. Plant it, and you will reap with great joy!

DAY AND NIGHT

The next step in the plan for victory given to Joshua was the instruction to meditate on the Word of God day and night. Instead of dwelling on the problem, meditate on the Word of God over the situation. To dwell means to stay in the same place, not to move from, or to be fixed in attention. All too often, we fix our attention on the problem, staying in the place of doubt and disbelief, but we are told to meditate on the Word of God! Day in and day out! When we do so, we won't have time to dwell on anything else. I am reminded just now once again of the scripture on our living room wall: *"You will keep in perfect peace all who trust in you, all whose thoughts are fixed on you!"* (Isaiah 26:3, NLT).

Meditate: "To dwell on anything in thought; to contemplate; to study; to turn or revolve any subject in the mind."[29]

Don't study the problem—study the Word of God! Keep the vision of God's promise before you. Revolve God's Word over in your mind, allowing *it* to occupy your thoughts instead of allowing the negativity of the enemy to take up residency in your thoughts and emotions. Every morning when you go to prayer, or during your devotional time with the Lord, take scriptures that relate to your situation with you. Read and *re*-read them, and declare them over yourself, your husband, and your marriage. Before going to bed at night, read them once again to keep your mind and heart focused on the Lord instead of whatever negativity may have transpired throughout the day. It is when we focus on the Word of God day and night that our way may be made prosperous, and that we will enjoy good success. Don't move from what God has already said about the situation, and when you've done all, stand on the Word of God.

> *For this reason, take up all the armor that God supplies. Then you will be able to take a stand during these evil days. Once you have overcome all obstacles, you will*

---

[29] *Webster's Dictionary 1828*, s.v. "Meditate," accessed December 21, 2023, https://webstersdictionary1828.com/Dictionary/meditate.

be able to stand your ground. So then, take your stand! (Ephesians 6:13–14a, GW)

Keep the Word before you night and day, and over time, you'll see a night and day difference in your situation.

WALK IN THE WORD

The third and final order given to Joshua was the command to *do* what was written within the Word. James 1:22 tells us, *"But don't just listen to God's word. You must do what it says. Otherwise, you are only fooling yourselves"* (NLT).

When the Word of God tells us to do good to and bless those who have brought us pain, then bless them. (Romans 12:14). When we are told not to retaliate when threatened, don't retaliate (1 Peter 2:23). Sow seeds of obedience and believe in faith for the harvest you are sowing for.

Be like Joshua and plant seeds of faith even before you see any sign of entering the land of promise. Show love to your husband, do good to him, treat him with respect. In this way, you are stepping out in faith to receive what you are believing for.

In Joshua 1:16 we find, *"They answered Joshua, 'We will do whatever you command us, and we will go wherever you send us'"* (NLT). They finally understood the necessity of obedience and were ready to obey whatever command they were given. They understood the connection of obedience and blessing. In my own life, God has shown me this principal in action. When I allow Him to move me by His grace to do the things He's asking of me, and yield to gentleness, kindness, and a meek attitude, He always meets me with a blessing that is greater than I had ever imagined. If God asks you to keep your mouth shut, keep it shut! If He asks you to apologize, then apologize. Nothing God asks of us ever goes without reward.

Hebrews 11:6 encourages us in this way: *"But without faith it is impossible to please Him, for he who comes to God must believe that He is, and that He is a rewarder of those who diligently seek Him."*

DECLARING THE VICTORY

As you sow the seeds of kindness and obedience, continue to call those things that be not, as though they are! Even if what you are confessing is not what you are seeing or experiencing at the time, continue to confess it anyway by faith. Look up Scriptures that speak the things you are asking the Lord for and pray them back to Him. God honors His Word even above His name (Psalm 138:2). What has God already said about your situation? If you don't have a personal Rhema Word from God on the situation, go to the Logos Word, the written Word of God, and make declarations from what He has already spoken in His Word concerning your marriage and your future. Make positive confessions over your husband. Make positive confessions over yourself concerning your attitude and/or disposition. Ask God to give you a gentle and quiet spirit. Make positive confessions over your marriage! Don't grow weary in well-doing, for you shall reap if you do not faint and give up, and God will reward you for your diligence.

REMEMBERING GOD'S DELIVERANCE

One of the ways we can keep from growing weary in the wait is to remember the goodness of the Lord. When the children of Israel crossed over the Jordan, they were told to build a memorial as a perpetual reminder of the Lord's goodness.

> *When all the people had crossed the Jordan, the Lord said to Joshua, "Now choose twelve men, one from each tribe. Tell them, 'Take twelve stones from the very place where the priests are standing in the middle of the Jordan. Carry them out and pile them up at the place where you will camp tonight.'"*
>
> *So Joshua called together the twelve men he had chosen—one from each of the tribes of Israel. He told them, "Go into the middle of the Jordan, in front of the Ark of the Lord your God. Each of you must pick up one stone and carry it out on your shoulder—twelve stones in all, one for each of the twelve tribes of Israel. We will use these stones to build a memorial. In the future your children will ask you, 'What do these stones mean?' Then you can tell them, 'They remind us that the Jordan River stopped flowing when the Ark of the Lord's Covenant went across.' These stones will stand as a memorial among the people of Israel forever"* (Joshua 4:1–7, NLT)

These are the stones God would have us build upon: stones of remembrance, reminding us of all that the Lord has done for us, all the past victories He has won for us, and the great lengths He is willing to go to bring about our deliverance. When we look ahead and only see walls of opposition, we can take a moment to look back at all God has done and be encouraged for the road ahead, remembering God's faithfulness to His Word. The road to deliverance is a process and will not happen overnight but is achieved in stages.

God began to deliver the children of Israel by sending their deliverer afloat in a basket daubed with pitch, set among bulrushes, positioning him for his destiny. He prepared him and sent him among them to bring them out of Egyptian bondage. He sent him to speak before Pharaoh, and to use the rod of God to reveal Himself to their oppressors and bring about their release. He parted the waters of the Red Sea and swallowed up their enemies, giving them relief from their struggles. He led them in the wilderness and brought them safely to the Land of Promise, once again opening waters at the Jordan to allow for their safe crossing. At each and every stage, they came closer to their desired destination.

Our deliverance too will be a process, but with each stride, God will bring us closer to the place of victory over our struggles and into a life of rest and harmony in the Land of Promise. But to attain it, we will need to be patient and must persevere. Psalm 27:13–14 encourages us in this way:

I would have lost heart, unless I had believed that I would see the goodness of the LORD in the land of the living. Wait on the Lord; be of good courage, and He shall strengthen your heart; wait, I say, on the Lord!

God did join me together with the perfect man for me, even though we have experienced some seasons of difficulty. God has remained faithful through it all. He has brought us through each and every storm and is making all the crooked paths straight. He has turned my sorrow into joy over and again, given me beauty for ashes, and has done exceedingly abundantly above all that I imagined, hoped for, and even asked for. He told me He would, and He did! He can do the same thing for you. We can have the breakthrough that we need if we will only believe. He's the great I AM, and He's able to do everything necessary to bring you to victory. How will He accomplish it? One step at a time.

Our day of deliverance can begin today if we will release our situation over to the Lord. If we do, we can be peaceful in the process of our journey into the Promised Land. Today can be the day that you give your situation over to the Lord. Today can be the day that you trust God with your life and your marriage. Today can be the first day on your path to healing and wholeness. Today can be your day of deliverance. Stand still and see the salvation of the Lord!

Deliver: "To free; to release, as from restraint; to set at liberty; as, to deliver one from captivity."[30]

SCRIPTURE CONFESSIONS

"Be strong and of good courage, for to this people you shall divide as an inheritance the land which I swore to their fathers to give them. Only be strong and very courageous, that you may observe to do according to all the law which Moses My servant commanded you; do not turn from it to the right hand or to the left, that you may prosper wherever you go. This Book of the Law shall not depart from your mouth, but you shall meditate in it day and night, that you may observe to do according to all that is written in it. For then you will make your way prosperous, and then you will have good success." (Joshua 1:6–8)

For this reason, take up all the armor that God supplies. Then you will be able to take a stand during these evil days. Once you have overcome all obstacles, you will be able to stand your ground. So then, take your stand! (Ephesians 6:13–14a, GW)

"You will keep in perfect peace all who trust in you, all whose thoughts are fixed on you!" (Isaiah 26:3, NLT)

---

[30] *Webster's Dictionary 1828*, s.v. "Deliver," accessed December 21, 2023, https://webstersdictionary1828.com/Dictionary/deliver.

Those who plant in tears will harvest with shouts of joy. They weep as they go to plant their seed, but they sing as they return with the harvest. (Psalm 126:5–6, NLT)

Dear Heavenly Father,

Please help me to be strong throughout this process. Help me to keep my eyes fixed on You, meditating on Your Word and Your promises both day and night. Please pour out Your grace upon me to be a doer of Your Word and not a hearer only, nor a forgetful hearer. Help me to keep Your Word on my lips instead of speaking what I see in the natural transpiring around me. Thank You, Lord, that even though I have sown in tears at times, You will cause me to rejoice in You as You bring about the harvest of blessing and victory in my life and in our marriage.

In Jesus' name, Amen.

Now to Him who is able to do exceedingly abundantly above all that we ask or think, according to the power that works in us, to Him be glory in the church by Christ Jesus to all generations, forever and ever. Amen. (Ephesians 3:20–21)

ADDITIONAL SCRIPTURE CONFESSIONS

Be anxious for nothing, but in everything by prayer and supplication, with thanksgiving, let your requests be made known to God. (Philippians 4:6)

And He answered and said to them, "Have you not read that He who made them at the beginning 'made them male and female', and said, 'For this reason a man shall leave his father and mother and be joined to his wife, and the two shall become one flesh'? So then, they are no longer two but one flesh. Therefore what God has joined together, let not man separate." (Matthew 19:4–6)

Father God in Heaven,

Thank You for bringing my husband and I together in marriage. Thank You for Your promise of becoming one. Please help us to let go of all things that would hinder the process of becoming one, giving proper place to You, each other, and our marriage. Help us to keep from allowing separation of any kind in our marriage, be it spiritually, physically, emotionally, or intimately. Keep us from allowing others, outside interests, or even ourselves to undo this beautiful gift of marriage You have given to us. Please help us to become one.

In Jesus' name, Amen.

But don't just listen to God's word. You must do what it says. Otherwise, you are only fooling yourselves. (James 1:22, NLT)

Dear Father God,

Thank You for Your loving care and help in our time of need and always. Please help both my husband and I not only to hear Your Word but to willingly and readily yield and submit to it, as it pertains to our marriage and in all things, being doers of Your Word on a daily basis.

In Jesus' name, Amen.

Let the word of Christ dwell in you richly in all wisdom, teaching and admonishing one another in psalms and hymns and spiritual songs, singing with grace in your hearts to the Lord. And whatever you do in word or deed, do all in the name of the Lord Jesus, giving thanks to God the Father through Him. (Colossians 3:16–17)

Dear Heavenly Father,

Please help my husband and I to pursue You and Your Word, seeking Your wisdom for our lives. Let Your Word dwell in us richly. Help us to encourage each other with Your Word and be patient with one another as You bring about the necessary changes within each of us.

Help us to be mindful of how we treat one another, being kind and loving instead of harsh and critical, as unto You, to bring honour to Your name. Help us to live in a manner that will glorify You in all that we say and do.

In Jesus' name, Amen.

For this reason we also, since the day we heard it, do not cease to pray for you, and to ask that you may be filled with the knowledge of His will in all wisdom and spiritual understanding; that you may walk worthy of the Lord, fully pleasing Him, being fruitful in every good work and increasing in the knowledge of God; strengthened with all might, according to His glorious power, for all patience and longsuffering with joy. (Colossians 1:9–11)

Father God in Heaven,

I come to You now, asking that You fill my husband and I with the knowledge of Your will for our lives. Please give us understanding of Your Word and of Your purpose and plans for our marriage. Lead us in Your Word to those passages that will wash us and cleanse us from the error of our way. Transform us into Your image by the renewing of our minds. Help us to be a light in this dark world instead of covering our light, behaving like the world. Help us to walk worthy of You, Lord, being fully pleasing to You in the manner that we behave toward one another. You have so graciously given us our marriage, and we desire good fruit from it.

I ask that You help us cut away those things that are draining and unproductive, and cause us instead to produce the kind of fruit in our marriage that will exemplify Your plan, purpose, and design for marriage. Please turn what the devil meant for evil into great good for Your Kingdom's glory. Please strengthen us as You accomplish the work within us, and help us to be patient with one another throughout the process.

In Jesus' name, Amen.

"No weapon formed against you shall prosper, and every tongue which rises against you in judgment you shall condemn. This is the heritage of the servants of the Lord, and their righteousness is from Me" says the Lord. (Isaiah 54:17)

Father God in Heaven,

Thank You so very much for Your love and concern for our marriage and for our happiness. Thank You for preventing the weapons the enemy has formed against our marriage to prosper. Please cancel out every negative word that has been spoken concerning our marriage, even those we have spoken ourselves. Help us to come into alignment with Your Word in all that we say, and speak only words of life over each other and over our marriage. Help us to simply keep silent in times when we would not speak in alignment with Your Word.

In Jesus' name, Amen.

The Lord will perfect that which concerns me; Your mercy, O LORD, endures forever; (Psalm 138:8a)

Dear Heavenly Father,

Thank You for caring about all that concerns us, and for perfecting all the things that will make for healing and wholeness in our marriage and in each other. Thank You for Your great mercy and loving-kindness toward us, and for Your everlasting faithfulness.

In Jesus' name, Amen.

Have you ever wanted a deeper relationship with the Lord but didn't know how to begin?

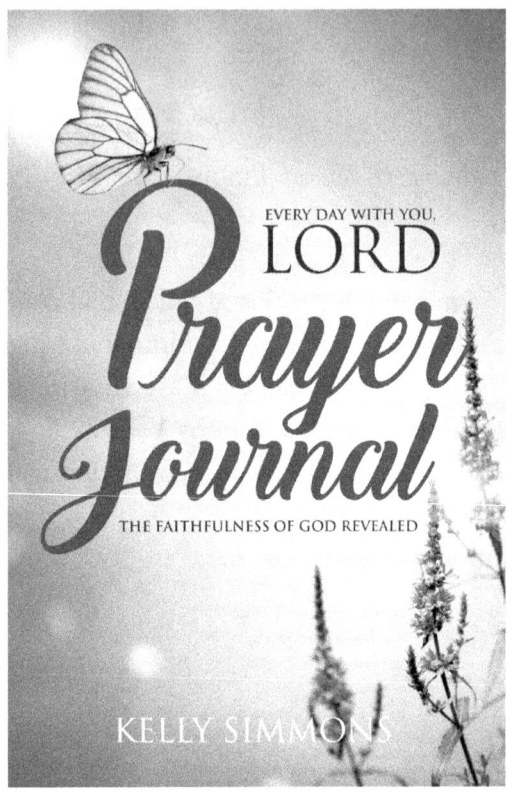

Every Day with You, Lord, Prayer Journal will lead you on a very personal journey to strengthen your prayer life, enhance your daily personal quiet time with the Lord, and help you experience for yourself, the faithfulness of God!

LOOK FOR IT SOON!

www.ingramcontent.com/pod-product-compliance
Lightning Source LLC
LaVergne TN
LVHW051601070426
835507LV00021B/2699